The Bay Area Homegrown Cookbook

Local Food, Local Restaurants, Local Recipes

By Aaron French

Photography by Elizabeth Tichenor and Aaron French

Voyageur Press

Contents

North of Market

The Mission & Points South

Oakland & Alameda

Berkeley, Albany & Walnut Creek

Foreword

"Wine is grown, not made," the mantra of the *terroir*-ists. Couldn't it also be said that cuisine is grown and not made, that cooking's raw materials, particular to people and place, determine the quality for better or worse of the finished dish?

What seems to me the greatest step forward in the development of American cuisine in the last thirty years is the acknowledgment of this principle. The manner and extent to which chefs far and wide have embraced it has become the measure of any kitchen of distinction.

I grew up in an Italian-American family in a suburb of San Francisco in a semi-rural neighborhood formerly planted with heirloom pears, concord grapes, mulberries, English walnuts, Seville oranges, and other uncommon citrus. Pineapple guavas ripened in the late fall, and after the first rains, bluets, yellow foot, and meadow mushrooms pushed through the leaves in the surrounding hills. My father planted Santa Rosa plums, apricots, apples, and mission figs in our backyard orchard. Between what was grown and found, there was fruit for every season, ripe for the picking. We shot rabbits and doves in the sugar beet fields near Sacramento and fished trout and crappie in the nearby freshwater lakes. For vegetables, we relied upon my grandmother's kitchen garden. Redolent garlic for our *bagna cauda* hung to cure in her backyard shed, and her signature carrots, stout sugar bombs, and bitter *cicoria* bore the scent of her soil and the mark of her mysterious green thumb.

With the benefit of such good fortune, I had already gained a natural education in the quality of food grown or gathered at closest hand. It wasn't until later that I realized that the taste and smells of my childhood had left me with a vivid taste memory, the requisite skill of any cook.

After college I packed up and moved to Italy to experience first-hand the traditions of the food of my childhood and to find my "voice" as a cook. I landed in the Tuscan countryside. Here was a place whose traditional *cucina povera* was formed by necessity upon ingredients intimately suited to its soil, its climate, to the needs of its people, its culture and ethos. It was a revelation to discover that here, food and place could not be separated.

I returned to take part in a major culinary awakening. Chez Panisse had been practicing for ten years the gospel of seasonality, of fresh, pure ingredients, and of local sourcing. I became the chef of the restaurant and was fortunate to be in the position to prod the efforts of our in-house forager to discover and vet a wide nexus of local farms. *Cuisine du marché* was the model, but we had gone the extra mile and eliminated the vendor in the middle. The nightly changing menu was derived from what we discovered in every season on any day. Often it changed in a moment with what came in the back door an hour before service.

The farm-to-table connection was also beginning to be forged through seminal events like the "Tasting of Summer Produce" and the steady proliferation of farmers' markets where chefs could not help but be drawn in by the seductive allure of tree-ripened fruit and vegetables just pulled from the earth. They met farmers and heard their stories, visited their fields, learned to taste their places. Those inspired by these lessons in naturalness could then drop their preconceived menu ideas and let the food they found do the talking.

Chefs now rely upon their farmer partners to provide the *raison d'être* of their menus. In those menus, farmers find a further ripening of the food they've grown and the fulfillment of their hard and risky work. This book is a testament to these vital relationships and to the momentous transformation that brings food—grown, raised, or gathered wild—directly to the table.

—Paul Bertolli, founder and chef, Fra' Mani Handcrafted Foods

Introduction

The chefs profiled in this book love to talk about food. More specifically, they love to talk about where they get their favorite ingredients. They all have stories about a particular dish that only comes alive at a certain time of year when their favorite farms offer up the perfect fruit or vegetable. At the same time, the farmers all told me stories about how much they love working with chefs. The chefs can give the farmers specific feedback about how their crops taste when prepared in different ways, and they can push the farmers to grow better, more diverse, and tastier crops.

This book was born from that synergy and could not exist without the unique contributions that these two committed groups of people bring to the food world. This connection is somehow both primal and new. The farmer–chef relationship is archetypal in form, and we can imagine the farmers of the ancient plains bringing in their harvests to the village hearth. While this transaction takes a different form now, the message remains the same: It is time to eat.

The local Bay Area harvest is amazingly diverse. The coastal farms are cool and verdant year round, creating superb conditions for tender greens, while the inland valleys bake in the summer sun, perfect ripening conditions for tomatoes. Because it will likely be eaten the next day, the farmer can pick that tomato at the perfect moment of ripeness and carry it gently to the restaurant door.

Again and again the chefs I interviewed told me it just makes sense to buy this local, great-tasting food, because people can taste the difference. Of course they can, but buying locally has many benefits beyond great taste. First and foremost, eating local food offers people a way to directly connect with their local environment. And we all know the phrase, "You are what you eat." Connecting with local farmers also means having a voice in how the surrounding countryside is managed: Is it properly cared for, pesticide-free, or perhaps organic? If you're not sure, your local farmer is only a short distance away— why not visit yourself?

In the meantime, let this book be your inspiration to learn about and cook some of the Bay Area's best local food and recipes, from the Bay Area's homegrown restaurants. Bon appétit.

North of Market

San Francisco, as famous for its food as for its steep hills, embraces the produce from coastal farms misted by the fog. Restaurants in the city's northern neighborhoods take full advantage of the Bay Area's vibrant food community, especially the chefs at these eateries found in Cow Hollow, Embarcadero, Pacific Heights, Jackson Square, and Alamo Square.

Betelnut Pejiu Wu

Chef Alexander Ong
Brookside Farm

"In the Bay Area, we're so progressive. When you talk about something as simple as recycling or composting, very recently the whole country was laughing at us and calling us hippies and idiots for doing these things, and now look—the rest of the country is catching up! And the bottom line is that you can actually make money by recycling," Chef Alex Ong says as he prepares a whole young pig for oven roasting. He presides over the kitchen at Betelnut Pejiu Wu, where he makes pan-Asian "street food" with an amazing commitment to local sourcing.

"With all the farms and resources available to us, it's only common sense for a chef to buy farm-to-table. I want my Asian cuisine to be 'authentic,' but does this mean I need to import all my ingredients from Asia? No way. I can be more authentic by getting from the local farms here, just as the vendors in Malaysia where I grew up got their green beans from the farm down the road."

"Food for us growing up was such an important part of daily life," Alex remembers about his Malaysian childhood. "We always knew, my sister and I, no matter what we were doing we had to be home for dinner at six every day!" His parents wanted him to be a doctor or lawyer, but when he graduated from high school, he decided that was enough school for him. After some traveling, he got a job as a banquet server at the Shangri-La Hotel in Kuala Lumpur. Eventually they let him start in the kitchen, where he worked for several years rotating through all the different stations, learning classical French, American, Japanese, and Malaysian techniques.

In 1988, Alex spent a year and a half working in Bermuda, where he entered a food competition "and won three gold medals." These awards were enough for him to get noticed, and three weeks later he flew to the United States for a job working in Atlanta at the Ritz Carleton. After a six-year stint spent moving around the country, Alex decided to settle down in the Bay Area. He started a "small restaurant project on Geary Street, and then went to work at the famed Stars Restaurant with Jeremiah Tower." It was there that he first "saw how to buy direct from farmers. It was amazing to work in Jeremiah's kitchen, learning about ingredient-driven food." After working at a variety of Bay Area restaurants, he was asked to work at Betelnut in 2001. One of his favorite farms to buy the restaurant's ingredients from is Brookside Farm, fifty miles away in Brentwood.

Brookside Farm is a true family operation run by Anne and Quong Tom and their son, Welling. Welling was three when his parents bought the ten acres he now farms with them. At the time, Welling says, his parents didn't want to be farmers; they just wanted to own a home with some land. But slowly the small garden they put in started to expand, and Anne found herself selling produce at local farmers' markets when it became too much to use at home. Welling went to UCLA but would return home for the summer breaks to work on the family farm and sell produce at the farmers' markets. During one of

these markets, he "realized it was possible to do something with the farm, that this might be my life's work." After college he returned with degree in hand to the land he grew up on. "I just couldn't imagine living anywhere else," he says with a soft smile. "This land is my home, and I need to take care of it so I can farm it forever."

The Toms grow an amazing variety of foods on their small plot of land, and do all the cultivation by hand. Until recently, Brookside Farm was largely a summertime operation, but eventually, the Toms decided to grow year round. "I have had to learn as I go, how to anticipate the weather so I can grow all year," Welling says. "At first I had to learn from some of the other farmers in the area. Some years I do better than others, and then sometimes I just get taken completely by surprise!"

Back in the Betelnut kitchen, Chef Alex talks about the shift in his customers' questions to him. "Now, people are asking us where our food is from, and we tell them. And then people can engage with us in the conversation about the food. So we don't print everything on the menu but hope to have a conversation with our customers."

"There's always more room to grow in what we are doing. I don't believe in there being an end of the road." As he hands me a plate of noodles, he says, "Try this. For me it comes down to cooking food you'd want to eat every day."

Emerald Fire Noodles

From Alexander Ong of Betelnut Pejiu Wu

6 servings

PART 1:

2 tbsp. vegetable oil
1 tbsp. minced garlic
1 tbsp. minced ginger
4 tbsp. red curry paste
1/2 c. fish sauce
1/2 c. oyster sauce
1 c. sugar
1/2 c. water
2 c. coconut milk

PART 2:

1 lb. spinach wheat noodles (chow mein), cooked and oiled
2 tbsp. vegetable oil
1 tsp. minced ginger
1 tsp. minced garlic
1 c. bean sprouts
1 tbsp. red Fresno chiles, cut into rings
1/4 c. mint or rau ram (Vietnamese mint), if available
1/4 c. basil leaves
1/4 c. garlic chives, cut in 2-inch pieces
1/4 c. cilantro leaves
1 tbsp. chopped roasted peanuts

Preheat a large wok or sauté pan. Heat the oil over medium heat. Add the ginger, garlic, and red curry paste, and cook for about 3–4 minutes, or until aromatic. Add the fish sauce, oyster sauce, sugar, water, and coconut milk. Bring the sauce to a boil and lower the heat to a bare simmer for about 5 minutes, to enhance the aroma.

Precook the spinach noodles in a pot of boiling water for about 4 minutes. The noodles should be tender but not overcooked. Drain and toss with a little bit of oil to prevent sticking. Preheat a wok. Add oil, then the ginger, garlic, sprouts, red Fresno chiles, and spinach noodles. Ladle in the sauce (not too much; you want to coat the noodles, not drench them). Finish the dish by tossing in the herbs until they are slightly wilted. Serve in a bowl (preferably a green one) with a sprinkling of chopped roasted peanuts.

Note: You can always substitute spinach pasta for the spinach chow mein.

Five-Spice-Salt-Roasted Chicken Salad

From Alexander Ong of Betelnut Pejiu Wu

4–6 servings

ROASTED CHICKEN:

1 whole "Mary's" organic chicken (approximately 3 lbs.)
1 orange
1 piece of ginger (approximately 2 inches)
1 small yellow onion
4 pieces of star anise
1/4 c. five-spice salt (see recipe below)
1/4 c. canola oil

FIVE-SPICE SALT:

2 tbsp. of each spice ground:
cinnamon
clove
fennel
star anise
Szechuan peppercorn
1/4 c. kosher salt

Mix spices with salt and set aside. Cut the orange and onion into quarters and smash the piece of ginger with the bottom of a small pot. Stuff the chicken with the orange, onions, ginger, and star anise. Tie the chicken's legs together with butcher's twine. Rub the chicken with the oil and five-spice salt. Roast the chicken at 350 degrees for about 45 minutes or until you reach a temperature of 150 degrees on a meat thermometer. Let the chicken rest outside the oven until cool enough to handle. Hand shred the meat and refrigerate. For best results use the chicken the same day.

PICKLED GINGER AND CHILES:

1 lb. Hungarian wax peppers (can substitute any medium hot chile)
1 lb. ginger
4 c. pickling liquid (see recipe opposite)

Slice the peppers into rings, keeping the seeds; set aside in a large bowl. Peel and slice the ginger paper thin on a Japanese mandolin. Wash the ginger three times in cold water to remove some of the starch. Drain the ginger and place in a large bowl. While the pickling liquid is still hot, pour half over the chiles and half over the ginger. Stir the chiles and ginger to make sure there are bunches sticking together. Let the pickles sit at room temperature until cool, then refrigerate. The pickles can last up to 2 weeks in the refrigerator.

PICKLING LIQUID:

2 c. white vinegar
2 c. sugar

Boil together until combined.

SPICY CASHEWS:

1/2 lb. cashews
1/8 c. water
2 tsp. chile powder
1 tsp. cayenne powder
2 tsp. sugar
2 tsp. salt

Toss the cashews with the water in a bowl until coated. Mix all spices and toss with the wet cashews. Spread on a sheet tray and toast in the oven at 350 for about 12 minutes, or until golden brown. Set aside to cool.

SESAME-SOY DRESSING:

1/4 c. white vinegar
1/2 c. chopped red onion
1/8 c. agave
1/4 c. tamari soy
1/2 c. sesame oil
1/2 c. olive oil

Put the vinegar, onion, agave, and soy sauce in a blender and blend on high. Slowly pour the sesame and olive oil into the blender while it's running (this will emulsify the dressing). To prepare the salad, place these ingredients on a platter in this order:

1 lb. wild arugula
roasted chicken meat
3 ripe pluots sliced thinly with the skin on
1/2 c. pickled chiles
1/2 c. pickled ginger
1 c. spicy cashews
sesame-soy dressing
cilantro to garnish

Boulette's Larder

Chef Amaryll Schwertner
Green Gulch Farm

"I started cooking back in the early 1970s while I was studying neuroscience in Austin. I had to work to pay tuition through school. And when I began to cook professionally, I realized that cooking was something for which I had a strong inherent knowledge," says Amaryll Schwertner. "Now, after thirty years, I know that there's no knowledge like the real experience I've gained over that time."

Her family had fled to the United States from Hungary when she was five, escaping the revolution. "We ended up in New York by mistake. Our food and language were all we could hang onto because every other part of our culture was lost."

"As a child," Amaryll says, "I wasn't consciously or directly interested in food, nor was I included. Children were not to be in the kitchen. But when I got up in the morning, my grandmother would have been up for hours making 'simple' things like risen doughnuts made from scratch." These experiences led to strong food memories that have stayed with Amaryll her entire life.

"I became a chef without any real training," she says. "Pretty early on when I came to the Bay Area, I became the chef at Mudd's in San Ramon, and we had our own ten-acre garden. And while that was great," she remembers, "I didn't want to be limited by that, so I started looking for other farmers to buy from as well. I would buy from Warren Webber at Star Route, and through him got to know about Green Gulch Farm—which was great because I was also studying Zen Buddhism at the time." Thirty years later, "I still shop from those same farmers."

The mission of Green Gulch Farm Zen Center, part of the San Francisco Zen Center, "is to awaken in ourselves and the many people who come here the *bodhisattva* spirit, the spirit of kindness and realistic helpfulness." Workers from the center sell produce to restaurants and in a stand at the Ferry Building Farmers' Market, but they do not sell to make a profit. Emila Heller came to Green Gulch back in 1974, "not quite at the beginning," she says. "We were young, traveling, following our nose, and we didn't have too many ideas at that time. I wasn't looking for a farm, particularly. Green Gulch wasn't really a farm back then, it was more of a garden in the beginning."

"Now, years later, I'll be seventy in a month and a half, so I'm not retired—I harvest and go to the market each week. I've already cycled through all the leadership roles over the years, and had tons of different titles that don't matter.

"We're not professionals at the farm," she clarifies. "The farm crew is no different than any other crew of people at Green Gulch. Everyone is a largely transient group, people come here to practice meditation. Most people come for less than a year, at most. But some, like me, never leave.

"For most people, the life can be tough. We rise at four in the morning to meditate, we study Buddhism, and we work hard in

the fields all day. We do this in a close community with other people, and then once a week we take our produce to the market and sell it to the world."

In particular, Green Gulch Farm is famous for its greens. "Our greens are amazing, due to our coastal climate and culture over the years. We know our crops and our soil, so we know what works. For example, we don't plant tomatoes, peppers, onions, or tarragon . . . sometimes our customers will ask us for something special—for example, Amaryll just asked us to grow some more escarole for her, and so we will honor that and plant some."

"My eyes tell me, each season, what I should be eating," says Amaryll, reflecting on having a farmers' market literally outside her restaurant door. Even so, she considers the way she works to be quite difficult—making a menu each day, based on what food is available at that time and place.

However, she is not exclusively a locavore. "I'm extremely aware of the seasonality of what I buy, but it's really, really important to not limit your choices. I do not limit my pursuit of ingredients to a hundred-mile radius. I get the best ingredients I can from all over the world, and the people involved in this are from all over, all kinds of people, and we make up an interesting community. It all comes together through food.

"So many things go into what food I choose to buy, and this hundred-mile food radius is a very simplistic picture. The idea of local food, in my opinion, is meant to be a cue to how to come closer to the source. Over the past thirty years, I've seen a very slow raising of awareness in general consciousness about the importance of food." But, like everything, she says, "It's complicated."

Lettuce Soup

From Amaryll Schwertner of
Boulette's Larder

The cool weather at Muir Beach is particularly beneficial to leafy greens. The lettuce varieties grown here are superb, whether sweet and tender or of the bitter green varieties. The exterior leaves of the lettuces make a lovely soup while of course the hearts fulfill their destiny as crisp salads, so loved that guests always comment on their flavor and vitality.

The lettuce leaves at the restaurant accumulate in greater volumes than would in a home kitchen, but this soup can be extended with other tender leaves and herbs as well as with potato or with celery root. In the fall I make it with apples and it is equally good with hen broth, roasted pork bone broth, or simply vegetarian. I'm presenting the vegetarian version here in deference to the vegetarian cuisine in the Green Gulch community.

Wash all of the outer leaves of lettuces. Slice thinly or brunoise six sweet onions or leeks. Wilt these in butter or oil until the onions are soft but not caramelized. Add the greens and then cover with pure water. Add sea salt and any other aromatics to taste (herbs like tarragon, parsley, chervil, or other odds and ends can be added, as well as soft greens like spinach). After 10–15 minutes, take the soup from the heat (the soup should come to a boil, then be turned down and quickly removed from the heat). Just before this point some enrichment may be added to the soup in the form of crème frâiche and perhaps some cooked potato. When the ingredients are cooked gently, the soup may be passed through a food mill or put into a blender to make it supple. Ice the ingredients if you can to preserve the color of the lettuces. The soup may be garnished with croutons or with a bit of cheese or lemon oil. It can be served warm or chilled.

Tian of Braised Broccoli Leaves

From Amaryll Schwertner of
Boulette's Larder

The giant broccoli wrapper leaves, very dark green and growing around the broccoli crown flowers, are of course also edible and rich in flavor and nutrients. I cook these in many ways at the restaurant, as well as the sweet wrapper leaves of cauliflower and the tops of many root vegetables, including carrots.

The tian, a clay oval cooking vessel in which the braised greens are topped with breadcrumbs and finished in the oven, is of rustic French origin. Use any open casserole that can withstand the oven.

Clean and trim the green leaves of their tough inner core vein. Blanch the greens in a large pot of boiling sea-salted water for 5 minutes, then drain. In a heavy-bottomed pan warm a few tablespoons of good olive oil, clarified butter, or a combination of browned butter and organic olive oil. (Meat fats can be used here, like duck fat or pancetta.) Sauté 2 tablespoons of minced garlic and three thinly sliced sweet onions until wilted and translucent. Add the blanched greens and cook for some slow and long period this time with salt. We also use a lovely dried Calabrian chili, which adds a bit of heat but not too much. Other seasonings of your choice may be added while the greens are softening.

Prepare an oval casserole with butter or oil, then place the soft greens into it. Season breadcrumbs (preferably levain) with olive oil and salt. Top the greens with the crumbs; a bit of crème frâiche or stock may also be added. Bake at 350 degrees until the crumbs are crispy. Sprinkle with grated Parmesan Reggiano if desired.

Center for Urban Education about Sustainable Agriculture

Chef Sarah Henkin

Dirty Girl Produce

"When you're at the market, you can't *not* be in tune with the seasons," exclaims Sarah Henkin. I first met Sarah, the market chef for CUESA's Ferry Plaza Farmers' Market, when I did a cooking demonstration for them one spring Sunday morning. Sarah's job, she told me, is to "help bring the food the farmers grow to life by creating cooked dishes visitors can eat and enjoy." She creates a market menu each week herself and brings in several guest chefs each weekend to give demonstrations using market produce. "It's all focused on seasonality. One of my favorite parts of my job is walking around with the other chefs on Saturday mornings doing the shopping, and being able to introduce them to all the farmers."

The Center for Urban Education about Sustainable Agriculture (CUESA) is a nonprofit organization created in 1994 to educate urban consumers and to create a vital link between urban dwellers and local farmers. CUESA has been managing San Francisco's Ferry Plaza Farmers' Market for over ten years, and Sarah Henkin has been a part of it for the last four. As she tells me, this same market was what "opened my eyes and made me want a career in food. But I knew I didn't want to be a restaurant chef, I wanted something different." After completing a degree at the California Culinary Academy, Sarah got an internship with CUESA and soon after became the Ferry Plaza Farmers' Market Chef.

"I love working with all the visiting chefs who come to shop. They have such a strong sense of loyalty, and many have been buying from the same farmers for years," she says. It seems, then, that CUESA's goal of bringing chefs, home cooks, and weekend warriors together with local farmers has been a huge success.

Though if you ask Dirty Girl farmer Joe Schirmer if he knew products like his dry-farmed tomatoes would be such a hit, he'd probably answer, "You never know what it's going to be like, I guess." This open-ended mentality may have stemmed from his earlier years growing up in Santa Cruz when he wanted to be a professional surfer. About his childhood he says, "You know the story, I was a surfer who wanted to be a gardener to save the world." As Joe grew up, he realized that being a surfer meant "being in the surf industry, which I wasn't into. I was just interested in surfing not the rest of it . . . so then what are you gonna do?"

"My grandfather grew up on a wheat farm in Kansas. Growing up, I was taught that farming was a total nightmare! My mom grew up being embarrassed to mention Kansas because our peasant roots were too shameful or whatever . . . but now, of course, it's cool," he smiles. "I never thought I'd want to be a farmer; growing up it was nasty, hard, and lame."

His father was a general contractor who taught him how to work with his hands, "fixing everything around." Though young at the time, Joe noticed that small-scale contractors didn't do so well. "I realized contracting was too risky and I should do something else."

So he got into farming. "When I started out, I was just grubbin', ready to throw my sleeping bag down in the corner of any field I could work in. I worked here and there, wherever I could learn something about the land. Now, years later, I need to think about preschool for the little one." And as owner of Dirty Girl Produce, Joe manages twelve people in the field, and another eight or so selling at his market stands. He's proud to say that when he first began farming Dirty Girl in 1997, they were only farming three acres. Now it's up to twenty-four, and still growing.

"The longer you're in it, the deeper you get into it and the more meaning you pull out of it," he told me. Joe comes across as a lighthearted, easygoing dude. He likes to talk about the reality of farming and getting rid of any misconceptions at the get-go. Yet, going from lifelong surfer to farmer, he's surprisingly optimistic about the whole thing.

Dirty Girl doesn't even pursue restaurants specifically. Joe figures some restaurants are going to like them and some aren't, so why try to convince them when your produce will do the talking?

"You just try to grow the best stuff you can, and restaurants will gravitate to you once they see that." It's true—as a chef myself, I like to try out new farms every week, but I can't help but scope out my favorite farm stands first as soon as I hit the morning market.

After speaking with Joe, I walk back around the restored Ferry Building that forms the center of the farmers' market, and look for Sarah in the CUESA kitchen. She looks up and smiles but doesn't stop talking with the crowd of eager customers who surround her for a sample of delicious food.

Dandelion Green and Delicata Squash Salad

Dandelion Green and Delicata Squash Salad

From Sarah Henkin of the Center for Urban Education about Sustainable Agriculture

6 servings

This is my favorite salad to serve at Thanksgiving—it makes good use of Dirty Girl's dandelion greens.

2 lbs. delicata squash
extra-virgin olive oil
kosher salt and freshly ground black pepper
1/4 lb. guanciale (or bacon or pancetta), medium to small dice
1/4 lb. dandelion greens, washed and dried
1/4 lb. salty, tangy cheese (feta or ricotta salata both
  work well)
1/2 c. pistachios, shelled, toasted, and roughly chopped
splash red wine vinegar

Preheat oven to 375 degrees. Cut squash in half lengthwise. Scoop out the seeds and slice the squash into thin half moons. Toss with olive oil, salt, and pepper and bake on a baking sheet until tender, about 15–20 minutes.

Heat a sauté pan over a medium-high flame. Add a glug of olive oil, heat until it starts to shimmer and circulate in the pan, then add guanciale. Sauté until crisp, then set aside to drain on a paper towel. Remove squash from the oven and let cool slightly. In a serving bowl, mix together the dandelion greens, half of the cheese, and half of the pistachios. Toss the squash in with the greens, add a splash of vinegar and a glug of olive oil over the top, just to coat the leaves, and gently toss to combine. Taste for seasoning and adjust, keeping in mind you will be adding more salty cheese. Garnish with the guanciale, remaining cheese, and nuts to serve.

Roasted Cauliflower, Radish, Mushroom, and Farro

From Sarah Henkin of the Center for Urban Education about Sustainable Agriculture

This makes a hearty side dish or salad; top leftovers with a poached egg for brunch on a cold day or puree into a soup.

1 1/2 cups farro, cooked
1/2 bunch radishes, perky greens still attached
olive oil
salt
freshly cracked pepper
1/2 pound cauliflower and/or romanesco
1/4 pound oyster mushrooms
1 clove garlic, thinly sliced
1/2 lemon
2 tablespoons fresh herbs, leaves picked and chopped—
  parsley, cilantro, thyme, savory, mint, whatever you prefer
splash red wine vinegar
soft, fresh goat cheese (optional)

Preheat oven to 425 degrees. Prepare the radishes by chopping off the greens, slicing them thin, and adding them to a container with plenty of cold water to wash. Wash the radishes well, dry, slice in half, and toss with a bit of olive oil, salt, and pepper. Set aside.

Prepare the cauliflower and/or romanesco: Slice off the hard ends of the stems. Chop into chunks about the same size as the radish chunks. Toss in a bowl with olive oil, salt, and pepper.

Prepare the oyster mushrooms: Wipe any dirt off with a clean kitchen cloth or paper towel. Toss in a bowl with olive oil, salt, and pepper. Either add all vegetables to their own baking sheets or put them all on one large baking sheet, keeping them in separate sections because they will finish at different times and will be removed from the oven separately. Place in oven and roast until vegetables are cooked through. Mushrooms will take about 10 minutes, radishes and cauliflower will take 15 to 20 minutes. Chop mushrooms once roasted and place all vegetables in one bowl.

While the vegetables are cooking, heat sauté pan over medium-high heat, add a splash of olive oil and garlic, and cook until garlic is tender. Add the radish greens and cook until wilted. Then squeeze in juice from the lemon and season with a pinch of salt. Add to the bowl with the roasted vegetables.

To finish: Toss cooked vegetables with cooked and drained farro. Add a splash of red wine vinegar, fresh herbs, and goat cheese, if using. Toss to combine. Taste and then add more salt, pepper, vinegar, or olive oil as needed. Serve.

Simple Creamy Swiss Chard Egg-Drop Soup

From Sarah Henkin of the Center for Urban Education about Sustainable Agriculture

6 servings

There aren't very many ingredients to this soup, so each of them has to be of the highest quality. Dirty Girl Swiss chard is so beautiful—it's absolutely impossible to walk by their farm stand and not buy a bunch.

4 c. chicken stock—preferably homemade dark chicken stock (trust me it makes a difference)
olive oil
2 thick slices country or sourdough bread, sliced into cubes
1 bunch Dirty Girl Swiss chard
1–2 cloves garlic, thinly sliced
sea salt
1/4 c. cream
2 farm-fresh eggs
2 tbsp. grated Parmesan cheese
squeeze of lemon
freshly cracked black pepper

Bring the chicken stock to a simmer and keep warm in saucepan until ready to use. Separate the leaves of the chard from the stems—save the stems for another use. Thinly slice the leaves or simply tear them into bite-size pieces. Wash the leaves well by covering with water in a large container. Set aside until ready to use.

Heat a sauté pan with olive oil and add the bread cubes. Toast on all sides until golden brown and set aside. The bread soaks up olive oil quickly, so you may have to add a splash more to the pan as they toast.

In a heavy-bottomed pot over medium-high heat, add a nice glug of olive oil. Add the garlic and cook until softened. Add the chard leaves, a pinch of salt, and the warm stock and simmer until the leaves are wilted. Add the cream and continue to simmer.

Crack the eggs into a small bowl and beat with a fork. Add the grated cheese and a pinch each of salt and pepper. Take the soup off the heat and quickly stir in the egg mixture. Continue to stir for about thirty seconds. The eggs will cook in the hot liquid; you should end up with egg strands, not chunks of scrambled egg. Add a tiny squeeze of lemon, taste and adjust seasoning with more lemon, salt, and/or pepper according to your taste. Divide between warm bowls, top with croutons, and serve.

Early Girl Tomato Bread with Burrata Cheese for One

From Sarah Henkin of the Center for Urban Education about Sustainable Agriculture

1 serving

This is so simple, it doesn't really need a recipe. If one of your very ripe tomatoes is accidentally crushed in your market bag, this is a good way to use it.

thick slice country-style bread
1 clove garlic, peeled
1 very ripe Early Girl tomato
glug very good olive oil
sea salt
sliced burrata cheese

Grill the bread or roast in a very hot oven until nicely toasted. Rub all over with the garlic clove. Cut the tomato in half and rub it all over the bread, pressing so that the tomato gives up all its juice and the bread soaks it up. Sprinkle with sea salt. Finish with a glug of olive oil and sliced cheese. Enjoy.

Nopa

Chef Laurence Jossel

Tory Farms

"I'm kind of the guy who doesn't want to be out in public," said Tory Torosian as he finally flopped down in front of me into a folding chair. I'd been bouncing questions off his back for the better part of fifteen minutes while he was eagerly chatting up customers, weighing out fruit, and keeping his sixteen- and ninteen-year-old sons occupied. The farmers' market is a regular family affair for the Torosians of Tory Farms. In fact, Tory's wife, Rebecca, has been working the Fresno market for over fourteen years.

It was family as well that brought Nopa's Jeff Hanak to the food scene. "It was having children and seeing how they eat. When we were growing up, my parents weren't aware of where things were coming from. They shopped at Safeway." Jeff grew up in Daly City, a suburb of San Francisco. Though Jeff remembers there always being farms nearby, the only farmers' market he remembers attending was the Alemany Market. Later, while working at Chow Restaurants, farmers' markets were all the norm. It was at Chow that Jeff met his current Nopa business partners, Laurence and Allyson Jossel.

It was during my interview with Laurence that I first learned about their rooftop herb garden: lavender, geraniums, rosemary—all are products of Jeff's passion for farming. The menu at Nopa changes every day, enabling the trio to just "go with the flow," a skill Laurence learned when he was just nine. A South African native, Laurence found himself in an entirely different community when his family moved to Houston, Texas. By the time he was fourteen, he got a job as a dishwasher, but he says, "It was a terrible restaurant . . . the equivalent of a Denny's." Hearing that coming from a chef who's worked at some of the most prestigious restaurants in the Bay Area made me wonder if the next great prodigy was the barista who served me tea that morning. . . . I should've left a bigger tip.

It was this same Laurence who, some years later after graduating from the California Culinary Academy in San Francisco, believed organic products would never be a bigger seller. "It's all very naïve," he had said during a conversation with his late mother-in-law, Diane Goodman, whom he calls the "Nopa Mom." With her, he would attend six farmers' markets a week, including the Wednesday market in San Francisco.

"I started buying dry-farmed tomatoes, and the more I used them, the less I had to use other ingredients . . . and darn that was a good soup," he reminisces. "That was a big turning point for me. The farmers are the heroes, let's just get that out of the way." Though for farmers like Tory, the real hero happens to be the dirt. "We're sitting on some ass-kicking soil! The best ground there is. The ground is the whole deal; it's what makes the fruit." Tory looks earnestly at me as he leans forward in his aluminum-framed chair amid the bustling farmers' market.

"Farming is horrible you know; the economics of farming are terrible. A lot of guys are going broke." Yet Tory Farms remains strong. The eighty-acre ranch, about two hundred miles south of San Francisco, is what the family endearingly calls "The Magic Ranch." Home to grapevines and stone fruit, the ranch is irrigated from a diverted portion of the King's River . . . and has been since the 1910s. "The neatest thing about our water situation is that we have few wells to run in the winter. Our district water comes from King's Canyon Gorge, coming right to the peach trees through gravity alone—ultimate low-tech!" Tory grins as he gets up and begins sorting through boxes of peaches. He continues to speak, hunched over and halfway under the market stand: "There's old cement pipelines from the 1940s, it's gravity fed all the way through the gate. We irrigate our entire farm without a stitch of plastic or a single bit of electricity."

"About a third of our ranch is wild habitat," he informs me. "Some of my neighbors might call that area my trashy weed patch. but it's full of quail, red-tailed hawk, kites, and even coyotes. It's beautiful! We don't mind if the regular birds come and eat our grapes." I muse over this steward of the land philosophy: caring for the wildlife, sharing your crop. Tory Farms isn't certified organic, but its owners wholeheartedly believe that their standards are much higher than those the organic label uses.

This is why Nopa has no issue purchasing non–certified organic stone fruit from Tory Farms. In fact, labels and origins, information that most restaurants in the Bay Area feel they must include, are deliberately absent from the menu cards. But part of Laurence's attitude on buying local and staying sustainable includes carrying all this out without the extra fuss.

"We just made [farm-to-table] the right thing to do, versus an exceptional way to do things. It's all really important to me; it's just not listed on the menu."

Corn Soup with Walnut Pesto

From Laurence Jossel of Nopa

6 servings

SOUP:

3 medium yellow onions, diced medium to yield 1 qt.

1/2 clove of garlic, sliced

1 jalapeno

3–4 tbsp. olive oil

salt

12 fresh basil leaves

10 medium ears of fresh corn, shucked to yield 1 1/2 qts.
 of kernels

1 c. cream

water as needed

Gently sweat the onions, garlic, and jalapeno in the olive oil until the onions are translucent, about 15 minutes. Season lightly with salt. Add the corn, the cream, and enough water to cover. Simmer slowly for about 20 minutes. Puree the soup and strain through a large-holed colander. Adjust the seasoning and serve with a dollop of the Walnut Pesto garnish and basil leaves.

WALNUT PESTO:

1/2 c. shelled walnuts

1 clove garlic

3 tbsp. grated Parmesan

1/2 c. extra-virgin olive oil

salt and cracked black pepper

10 fresh basil leaves

Combine all ingredients except the basil in a food processor and puree until smooth. Add the basil and puree quickly, keeping in mind that the basil will turn brown if blended more than necessary. Stir in salt and pepper to taste.

Corn Soup
with Walnut Pesto

Olive Oil–Poached Albacore Tuna

From Laurence Jossel of Nopa

6 servings

6 tbsp. whole cumin seeds
6 tbsp. whole coriander seeds
6 tbsp. whole fennel seeds
1 tsp. chili flakes
1 tbsp. salt
1 1/2 lbs. albacore tuna, trimmed of any skin, membrane, and bloodline
2 qts. extra-virgin olive oil, or more as needed to cover

Toast the whole spices in a dry pan until fragrant. Let them cool slightly, then grind and combine with the chili flakes and salt. Cut the fish into 2-inch cubes, then dredge in the seasonings to coat all sides. Once seasoned, let it sit for 12–24 hours. In a pot over medium heat, slowly bring the olive oil up to 225–250 degrees. Gently place the tuna in the oil and poach for one minute, keeping it rare in the center. Place the poached cubes in a deep dish. Let the olive oil cool to room temperature and pour it back over the tuna. The tuna can be stored this way in the refrigerator for up to three days.

To serve, carefully remove the tuna from the oil and serve around room temperature. We like to serve the tuna in the style of a Niçoise salad: room temperature with some combination of the following accompaniments:

boiled potatoes, tossed with lemon juice, parsley, and salt
roasted red peppers, peeled, cut into strips, and marinated in sherry vinegar
hard-cooked eggs, halved lengthwise
marinated whole olives
blanched haricots verts
ripe summer tomatoes, cut into bite-sized wedges
a dollop of aioli
pickled vegetables, such as red onions or beets
lightly dressed greens

Summer Melon Salad

From Laurence Jossel of Nopa

6 servings

At least 3 ripe melons of different varieties, cut into 1 1/2-inch cubes to yield 6 c. (see note below)
1 bunch fresh mint
1 1/2 c. cubed feta cheese
1/2 c. kalamata olives
very fresh extra-virgin olive oil
sea salt and freshly ground black pepper

Note: Use melons of at least three different colors and textures, such as:
Jimmy Lee or Red Crimson watermelon (red, crisp)
Yellow Doll watermelon (yellow, crisp)
Sharlyn, Charentais, or Crenshaw (orange, soft)
Honeydew (green, soft)

Tear off the mint leaves and combine all solid ingredients, taking care to avoid excess moisture. Gently toss in olive oil, salt, and pepper to taste.

Quince

Chef Michael Tusk
Tomatero Farm

As we sit in the lounge area of the acclaimed Quince restaurant, Chef Michael Tusk returns from the farmers' market, excited to show me some golden raspberries he's just bought to serve with desert that evening—and he starts talking about the look and feel of the restaurant he's created. "You don't know immediately who you are going to be when you open as a restaurant," he notes. Restaurants are always changing: from the menu to the staff to the supplier. Mike continues, "As a chef, you're never quite happy with how you're cooking at the moment—it's an inner struggle to have enough of a conscience to be consistent but also not to be something you're not. So every year, you try to turn it up a notch."

In California especially, guests are becoming increasingly food savvy, and they don't hesitate to ask for the origin or variety of certain ingredients. "I kind of feel like if you're at a certain quality of restaurant, it's a given that you should be ordering and buying from solid small farmers. That's what people expect these days when they come from the Bay Area."

Chef Mike spent his early years in New Jersey, and "eating was a big part of growing up." He went to New Orleans to study art history at Tulane and started working in restaurants. "There was a lot of food culture that was historic, and that definitely was seasonally driven from the get-go." He was also inspired by the "great quality of the markets in the French Quarter, and lots of music and art, and eating."

He decided to enroll at the Culinary Institute of America to develop his passion for food further, and upon graduation he went to Europe to work in the kitchens of Italy and France. But the big turning point for his passion for farm-to-table cooking was working with Alan Tangren at Chez Panisse. "He was an encyclopedia of knowledge of where to get things from. I would ask, 'Where can I get organic this or organic that?' and he would always point me in the right direction, whether it was a larger organic farm or small-scale family farm or from the back of a truck."

Mike considers himself a realist, trying to stay as local as possible yet loyal to his farmers from farther away. "There's no turning back now—the products at the farmers' markets look so much more vibrant, and there's so much more awareness here." In addition, Mike insists that shopping at small weekday markets is key to keeping the neighborhood restaurants different.

It was in one of these markets that he met Adriana Silva from Tomatero Farm. "She's one of the new wave of farmers who are offering great quality for great prices, and I think it works well for the restaurant and for the farmers themselves to build these relationships."

"And," he adds, "She grows these amazing golden raspberries that I just can't get enough of!"

These new young farmers have also learned the importance of building lasting relationships with workers. That's why Tomatero Farm prides itself on its fair wage practices. "We farm year round, not necessarily because it makes us money, but because it keeps everyone employed. We certainly don't make money in the winter. From solely a financial outlook, we should just grow summer crops and get out of there." The farm currently supports thirty-five employees full time, a large scale compared to its humble beginnings.

"The farm started with a credit card and a borrowed tractor in 2002. I kind of just fell into it, really." Adriana had little prior farm experience. "Well, I worked for a few other farms, briefly," she says, "but I was drawn to the fact that everyone respected farmers and that farming was a necessary and core business that's sustainable."

Her partner, Chris Tuohig, has a similar story. He drove by Live Earth Farm in Watsonville one day and decided to take a tour. "I took a tour of the farm, and the next day I started looking for farms that were hiring." After working on a farm in Davenport for a few months, he was able to buy his first four acres of land. That number has since grown to sixty acres, with such crops as strawberries, tomatoes, and greens. With a strict crop-rotation schedule, about forty acres are always in production, keeping the farm's workers employed year round.

Adriana and Chris share most of the farm duties, but some tasks just get naturally segregated. "He does more of the heavy work," she says with a laugh, "which leaves me with the boring work like bookkeeping and all of that." But they are both in the dirt planting, weeding, and harvesting, and at the markets selling their produce.

The three of us walk along rows of tomatoes, slowly ripening in the warming sun, and come upon a field of low bushes. "And these are why you're here—our golden raspberries," Adriana says as she picks a berry and reaches out to hand it to me. Simply perfect.

Tomatero Farm
Black Cabbage Sformato
with Parmigiano Reggiano Fonduta

From Michael Tusk of Quince

6 servings

2 oz. butter

3 oz. flour

1 pt. whole milk

1 lb. Tomatero Farm black cabbage, destemmed (you can substitute dinosaur kale or cavolo nero)

1 c. Parmigiano Reggiano, grated

1/2 c. extra-virgin olive oil

2 whole eggs

1 egg yolk

Parmigiano Reggiano Fonduta (see recipe on facing page)

Preheat an oven to 350 degrees. Melt the butter in a 2-qt. saucepot. Add the flour and stir over moderate heat to make a roux. Reserve the roux.

In another 2-qt. saucepot, bring the milk to a boil. Add the cabbage and cook until tender. Remove the cabbage and strain the hot milk into the pot with the roux. Whisk constantly to make a bechamel base for the sformato. Pour the hot bechamel into a blender and add the reserved cabbage, Parmigiano Reggiano, olive oil, whole eggs, and yolk. Blend over high heat until smooth. Season to taste.

Butter six 8-oz. ramekins and pour in the sformato base. Cook the uncovered ramekins in a boiling water bath in the oven for about 40 minutes or until barely set (a cake tester should come out dry). Invert the sformatos onto hot plates and drizzle extra-virgin olive oil over them, then pour Parmigiano Reggiano Fonduta over the sformatos. Garnish with Tomatero Farm oven-dried Early Girl tomatoes.

PARMIGIANO REGGIANO FONDUTA:

1 c. vegetable stock
1 c. heavy cream
1 c. Red Cow Parmigiano Reggiano, grated
salt and nutmeg

Combine the stock and heavy cream in a 1-qt. pan and reduce by half. Add the grated cheese and blend with a hand mixer or in a blender. If the fonduta is too thick, add a little vegetable stock until a nice smooth consistency is achieved, and season with a pinch of salt and hint of nutmeg to taste.

Tataki Sushi and Sake Bar

"Sustainability Guru" Casson Trenor and Chef Kin Lui
Wild Planet Seafood

Tataki Sushi is the first sustainable sushi restaurant in the United States. This is a huge thing to say, since the sushi industry is notoriously hostile when it comes to environmental issues. The top five sushi species are all facing rapid population decline, and everyone said it would be absurd to open a sushi restaurant without those species on the menu.

The owners of Tataki, Kin Lui and Raymond Ho, decided to do it anyway, opening their doors on February 2008. To date, Tataki has eliminated bluefin (toro), farmed salmon (sake), imported King crab (kani), yellowtail (hamachi), octopus (tako), and even the popular freshwater eel (unagi) from its menu.

They began showing the public that it was possible to have a memorable and tasty restaurant experience by trying new flavors without just resorting to the old, unsustainable sushi favorites. Their rich array of menu items includes favorites such as their Scallop Tataki: a flavorful rendition of seared Hokkaido scallops, citrus aoli, rice crackers, and lemon zest. Who would go back to ordering plain unagi nigiri after that?

Okay, admittedly unagi is delicious and the owners of Tataki know that. So if you really, really can't give it up, the owners have agreed to compromise. Because of the crashing decline in eel populations, and the popularity of unagi nigiri on any Japanese menu, they've come up with their own version: Faux-Nagi.

As Tataki's "Sustainability Guru" Casson Trenor points out, "When you eat the unagi, you just taste the rest of it—you don't usually taste the eel, you taste the rice and sauce and get the eel texture. So we use a local sustainable fish [wild U.S.-caught black cod] and cook it in a special way to simulate the texture of the eel. . . . It took us maybe three months to get the right fish and to figure out how to cook it, and it took a while to make it taste the way it does now."

Not surprisingly, Tataki also has a delicious vegetarian menu, with options not normally offered at other sushi restaurants. Casson firmly believes, "You don't have to eat seafood to have a lovely meal."

The Tataki chefs strive to walk the talk of sustainability. Most recently, they cut yellowfin tuna off the menu and brought in local pole-caught albacore to replace it. But this created another problem, says Casson. "The local pole-caught albacore was trimmed better and therefore didn't have the 'trim' extra to make the spicy tuna roll—and so we went to the producer and asked for more trim that the producer was throwing away."

That producer is Wild Planet Seafood, based in McKinleyville, California, with local seafood operations up and down the Pacific coast.

"From small beginnings come great things," says Bill Carvalho, founder and "chief mission advocate" for Wild Planet Seafood. In 2002, while standing in the Monterey Bay Aquarium, Bill had an epiphany that caused him to change his entire life's work.

Bill, the grandson of Portuguese immigrants, grew up in the logging and fishing town of Arcata in Northern California. Seafood was a part of everyone's life, he tells me. While Bill was growing up, the entire family would fish for smelt on evenings and weekends during the season, and it was just "in my blood," he says. But he didn't join the seafood business until 1990. "I turned to the seafood industry as something that I loved and something that I wanted to be involved in." He founded Carvahlo Fisheries, which ran a few boats but also bought and distributed fish from other operations.

Over the intervening years, Bill came to realize the serious peril that the seafood industry was in: problems with harvest methods, problems with fish stocks, systemic problems with business practices. One day, standing in the Monterey Bay Aquarium, he saw an educational display about the decline of global ocean health, and he realized that his business was part of the problem. He knew that if things continued, he'd be out of a job as fish populations continued their worldwide decline.

In 2002, Carvallo Fisheries drew a line in the sand and went green. The company began fishing and selling only sustainable food species, which "was certainly a backwards move to do in the short term, as is any environmental move in the right direction globally." By 2004, Bill had created Wild Planet Seafood as a separate brand to signal his commitment to sustainability.

The new brand slowly grew but still needed support from the parent company, so Bill started looking for outside funding to stabilize his new project. In 2008 they attracted the attention of Sea Change Management, a private equity fund founded, in part, by the Packard Foundation. For Bill, this brought him full circle, back to that afternoon in the aquarium when he had his epiphany. The same Packard Foundation that stabilized his new sustainable seafood company also founded the Monterey Bay Aquarium where he had stood gazing at the endangered fish.

Tataki Sushi and Sake Bar's Extinguisher Roll

From Kin Lui and Raymond Ho of
Tataki Sushi

Makes 1 sushi roll

2 oz. pole-caught North Pacific albacore, finely chopped
2 oz. pole-caught North Pacific albacore, cut into
  1/4-inch cubes
1 tsp. red chili sauce (we prefer Sriracha Hot Chili Sauce)
1 sheet roasted nori seaweed
freshly prepared sushi rice
1/4 cucumber, peeled and cut into small strips
1/2 avocado peeled and thinly sliced
spicy mayo sauce (1/4 tsp. red chili sauce with 2 1/4 tsp.
  Japanese mayo—we prefer Kewpie Mayo)
1 tsp. of habanero masago (capelin roe)

Mix both the finely chopped and cubed albacore with the red chili sauce. Cut the nori sheet in half and lay it on a cutting board. Dampen your fingers in water and spread a thin layer of sushi rice evenly over the seaweed, leaving a 1/2-inch gap on the top and bottom. Turn the seaweed with the rice over so that the rice is on the bottom and the nori is on the top. Spread the albacore mixture lengthwise and thin cucumber slices evenly on the nori.

To roll the sushi: Slowly fold the end of the nori closest to you over the filling and tuck it in. Use a bamboo mat to seal and compact the filling. Place avocado slices perpendicular on top of the sushi roll, overlapping every 1/4 inch on each slice. Place plastic wrap over the avocado and use a bamboo mat to bond the avocado to the sushi rice. Keep the plastic wrap on the avocado to avoid any sticking when slicing the roll. Slice the roll into eight equal pieces.

Display on your favorite plate. Squirt a small amount of spicy mayo sauce on top of each piece of sushi (you can control the amount of heat here). Add the habanero masago evenly on top of the spicy mayo sauce.

Tataki's "Faux-Nagi"

(OUR SUSTAINABLE REPLACEMENT FOR *UNAGI*, OR FARMED FRESHWATER EEL)

From Kin Lui and Raymond Ho of Tataki Sushi

6 servings

3 lb. fillet "best choice" sablefish
sea salt
sake
2 pieces konbu
1/2 c. soy sauce
1/2 c. sugar, or appropriate substitute (stevia, for example)
3 tbsp. mirin
3 tbsp. sake
1 handful katsuobushi (hook-and-line caught skipjack flakes)
3 tbsp. water
potato starch
extra water
sesame seeds

Dust both sides of the sablefish fillet with sea salt. Wrap in cellophane and refrigerate for 15–20 minutes. Remove the fillet and unwrap. Wash the salt off the fillet with very cold water. Blot dry with a paper towel.

Wet a new paper towel with sake. Use this towel to moisten the konbu. Sandwich the sablefish between the two pieces of sake-moistened konbu. Wrap in plastic and refrigerate for 30–40 minutes. Unwrap, remove the konbu, and return to the refrigerator.

Mix the soy sauce, sugar, mirin, sake (3 tbsp.), katsuobushi, and water (3 tbsp.) in a saucepan. Bring to a boil, lower heat, and simmer for about 10 minutes. Drain and remove katsuobushi. Set the soy/mirin sauce aside.

In a small bowl, combine cold water and potato starch at a 4:1 ratio. Stir to create a thickener. Return the soy/mirin sauce to a boil, then lower heat to a simmer. Add the potato starch thickener to the soy/mirin sauce little by little as necessary until desired consistency is reached. Remove from the heat and let cool.

Slice sablefish into portions (as appropriate for nigiri, sashimi, or whatever dish is being served. Lightly char one side of the fish with a small butane torch (or sear very briefly in a hot saucepan). Top fish with a drizzle of the soy/mirin sauce and a sprinkle of sesame seeds. Serve atop rice or as desired.

The Mission
& Points South

Although the southern part of San Francisco might be best known for its history, it also holds a number of award-winning restaurants. In the neighborhoods south of Market Street, particularly the Mission District, Noe Valley, Potrero Hill, and Dogpatch, chefs are creating dishes with local, homegrown ingredients that make diners want to return again and again.

Contigo

Chef Brett Emerson
Tierra Vegetables

Contigo, run by husband-and-wife team Brett and Elan Emerson, opened in the spring of 2009 and already has a loyal following. Contigo's Spanish-influenced menu is a world away from Brett's childhood in Southern California. Growing up, the food his mom cooked was the product of the convenience foods of the 1960s and 1970s. "Don't get me wrong," he said, "My mom was a great cook, it was just coming from a different era." It was only in the summers, Brett remembers, that they would go to a local farm stand for sweet corn and strawberries. "There was such a difference between that summer farm-stand food and the food that we would normally eat. That was something I really noticed growing up."

Brett studied international relations at Georgetown and imagined a career in law, but a short stint working as a legal assistant in a law firm ended that dream—he hated it. He moved to San Francisco and started teaching environmental education, but increasingly his heart was with the food he was eating. He was particularly blown away by the produce at the Ferry Plaza Farmers' Market. "Within two years of moving to San Francisco, I started culinary school."

An internship at Chez Panisse was pivotal for him. He formed a strong connection with Chef Russell Moore, and long after his time there was over, he would spend his Saturdays in the Chez Panisse kitchen, with Russ giving him dishes to work on to improve his cooking. And all the while he was building relationships with growers at the Ferry Plaza Farmers' Market, farmers like Lee and her brother, Wayne James, of Tierra Vegetables.

Brother and sister Wayne and Lee James have been farming together since the mid-1970s. The Jameses' parents were avid gardeners, and when a family friend bought forty acres in the Potter Valley, Wayne went to work for him. This was right at the beginning of the farmers' market movement, and when the first market opened in Santa Rosa, Wayne realized that "this was a great way to sell—you could sell what you had, and not have to deal with supplying the wholesale markets."

A few years later, in 1980, Wayne and Lee approached a neighbor who had three unused acres and asked to be able to farm it. They agreed on a lease price of a hundred dollars per acre for the season.

Wayne and Lee set out earnestly clearing the weeds and planting their crops for sale. A few months later the landholder came back, saying, "I've thought things over, and we're going to have to renegotiate the lease." He lived across the way and liked the view so much he wanted to reduce the price to free. Ultimately, Lee and Wayne started to look for more land, moving around until they landed on seventeen acres on the north edge of Santa Rosa in 2002.

During this time, Wayne studied viticulture and worked in the vineyards before joining the Peace Corps for a time. Lee, for her part, studied fisheries management at Humbolt State University, and worked for the California Water Quality Control Board.

Originally they sold at farmers' markets for the vast majority of their sales but didn't necessarily have a great sense of valuing their time. "We would spend hours and hours bunching beets," Lee says, "and then end up selling them for twenty-five cents a bunch."

"Once we opened up the farm stand next to our farm we dropped most other markets, and we're still doing fine. The local community is really supporting us." In addition, they currently sell to about fifteen restaurants in San Francisco regularly, and another five or so in Santa Rosa.

"Some chefs love our very specific things that other growers don't have, such as varieties of hot chilies, parching corn, et cetera." And this is why Brett and Elan over at Contigo love them so much. Contigo's fare is exciting, and spices including Tierra Vegetables' peppers play a vital role in mixing things up.

Tierra Vegetables grows over fifty varieties of pesticide-free chilies. Pesticide-free, but not certified organic. "I don't want the feds telling us how to grow stuff," Lee said one afternoon. "We've always been 'organic' by style, but we were never into the movement, never into following certain rules. And since we never did it in the beginning, we certainly wouldn't do it now. It just sounds like such a pain, and we already spend too much time on the computer!" Certifications aside, the quality of their produce attests to the care they take growing their crops.

"Her chiles are a real splurge," Brett says. "They're so special and unique that you really take care when you use them, and our customers can taste it."

Since Contigo's inception, Brett has been shopping the markets and building relationships that mean a lot to him. The most important thing, he says, is that "I know the face of everyone who contributes food for my restaurant. Yes, it's a business, but the more important thing is that it's the story of people told through the food."

Local Ling Cod with Romesco Sauce and Spring Vegetables

From Brett Emerson of Contigo

6 servings

2 lbs. ling cod fillets or other firm white fish, such as halibut

sea salt

2 c. sugar snap peas

12 spears medium asparagus

1/2–1 c. fish stock, preferably made from the ling cod bones

2 c. romesco sauce

sherry vinegar

4 tbsp. extra-virgin olive oil

1 clove garlic, minced

2 c. pea shoots

few drops lemon juice

Remove any pin bones from the ling cod fillet and cut into six equal pieces, about 5–6 oz. each. Season ling cod fillets with salt and let sit about 30 minutes—seasoning the fish with salt helps to firm up the flesh of more delicate fish, like ling cod. Set aside and prep the vegetables.

Remove the strings and ends of the snap peas with your fingers. Cut in half on a bias. Bring a pot of water to a boil, add salt to the water, and blanch the snap peas for about a minute. They should still be crisp. Remove peas from pot and set aside.

Peel the lower half of the asparagus spears and snap off the fiber-ous bottom ends. Cut asparagus into 1/4-inch pieces on a bias, but leave the tips whole. Blanch the tips in the same pot that you cooked the snap peas. Remove when crisp tender, after about 1 minute, and combine with snap peas.

Combine 1/2 c. of the fish stock and the romesco sauce in a small pot. Bring to a simmer. Taste and season with salt. Taste the sauce as well—if it needs more acidity, add a few drops of sherry vinegar. The sauce should be bright and lively, yet nicely balanced. The flavor of the chiles and nuts should dominate. Also check the consistency of the sauce. It should have the thickness of a cream or butter sauce, but not be as smooth. If it is too thick, add more fish stock and adjust the seasoning again.

Heat a large cast-iron pan over medium high heat for 2–3 minutes. Pat the fish fillets dry. When the pan is smoking hot, add 2 tbsp. of the oil, then the fish fillets, presentation side down. Cook for a couple of minutes on each side until the fish flesh has started to firm up and the fish is just opaque in the center.

Meanwhile, heat a large sauté pan over high heat. When the pan is hot, add 2 tbsp. of the oil, then add the sliced asparagus. Sauté the asparagus for a minute, then add the minced garlic to the pan and continue to sauté and toss until the asparagus is lightly caramelized and tender, another minute. Add the snap peas and asparagus tips and toss until all the vegetables are heated through. Season with salt.

Ladle the sauce in a circle onto a plate or large shallow bowl. Place a large spoonful of the vegetables in the center of the sauce. Lay the cooked ling cod on top of the vegetables. Toss the pea shoots with a pinch of salt and a few drops each of lemon juice and olive oil. Top the fish with a small tuft of pea vines before serving.

Calamars a la Planxa with Tolosa Beans, Sofregit, and Allioli

From Brett Emerson of Contigo

6 servings

- 2 c. dried Tolosa beans or other small black or white bean, soaked overnight
- 1 onion, peeled
- 1 carrot, peeled
- 3 cloves garlic, peeled
- 3 sage leaves
- 2 medium tomatoes
- 1/4 tsp. pimenton de la vera, dulce (sweet smoked Spanish paprika)
- 3 lbs. fresh squid, cleaned, bodies and tentacles separated
- coarse sea salt, such as Portuguese flor de sal
- extra-virgin olive oil
- 1/2 c. Allioli (see recipe below), thinned with a little water to the consistency of heavy cream
- small handful of baby cress, such as ancho cress
- few drops of lemon juice

First, cook the beans, drain, and add to a small pot. Add enough water to cover by 1/2 inch. Bring to a simmer, skimming foam that rises on top. Cut the onion in half. Reserve one half for the sofregit, and add the other half to the bean pot, along with the carrot, two cloves of garlic, and the sage leaves. Slowly simmer over low heat until the beans are very tender and creamy but not falling apart, about 1 1/2 to 2 hours. Add a splash of olive oil in the last 15 minutes of cooking time. Allow beans to cool in their liquid.

While the beans are cooking, make the sofregit. Heat 2 tbsp. oil in a pan over medium-low heat. Add the onions and cook slowly until they turn translucent, about 30 minutes. Mince the remaining clove of garlic and add to the pan. Continue cooking and stirring, about 10 more minutes, until the onions become pale golden. Cut the tomatoes in half and grate, flesh side down, on the largest holes of a box grater. You should be left with just the tomato skins. Discard skins and add the grated tomato and the paprika to the onions. Continue to cook until the tomato breaks down and separates from the oil, about 10 more minutes.

Drain the beans, reserving 1/2 c. of the cooking liquid. Combine the beans and the sofregit in a small pot and bring to a simmer. Add some of the reserved cooking liquid if necessary. Season with salt.

Heat a large cast-iron skillet over high heat for 2–3 minutes until smoking hot. Sprinkle the pan with coarse sea salt. Lay the squid bodies on top of the salt. Do not crowd the pan. Drizzle the squid with a few spoonfuls of oil. They should sizzle and begin to nearly smoke. Cook about 2 minutes per side, until the squid turns golden brown, the color of cornflakes. Transfer to a small bowl and sprinkle with a little lemon juice and olive oil. Check the seasoning.

Spoon a few beans onto a plate. Top with squid bodies and tentacles in a row. Pour over some of the juices released by the squid. Drizzle with Allioli. Toss the cress with a few drops each of lemon juice and olive oil. Top each portion of squid with a pinch of the greens.

ALLIOLI:
- 2 cloves garlic
- sea salt
- 1 egg yolk, at room temperature
- 1–3 tsp. lemon juice
- 1 c. best-quality extra-virgin olive oil, preferably Arbequina

In a mortar, pound garlic to a paste with a pinch of salt. Transfer to a bowl. Add the egg yolk and a tsp. or two of lemon juice. Beat mixture with a whisk while slowly drizzling with olive oil.

Delfina

Chefs Craig Stoll and Matthew Gandin (pictured)
Star Route Farm

"We're not out there trying to change how the world eats, we're just trying to buy and create good food." This statement is at the core of how Craig Stoll operates his restaurant.

"It's all so simple now," says Craig, chef and owner of Delfina. "Basically we buy stuff and make something out of it." Craig and Annie Stoll make it seem just that simple with their growing assortment of ever-popular restaurants. They opened their first restaurant, Delfina, in 1998. It became so popular that they doubled its size a year later. In 2005 they opened a pizzeria next door, adding a third restaurant in 2008. In fact, as I write this, they are working on opening their fourth restaurant in the spring of 2011.

Craig outlines his menus monthly, in broad strokes, "but things really change all the time. You have to be ready to improvise."

Craig takes his passion for quality ingredients to an exacting degree—buying from specific farmers who grow different varieties of vegetables that are good for specific dishes he creates. "I've been friends with some of our farmers for over twenty years, since I was a prep cook at Compton Place." That was back in 1988, and by that time Craig had already graduated from the Culinary Institute of America in New York and Florida International University in Miami with a degree in hospitality management.

In fact, it was at Compton Place where Craig learned to cook the way he does now. Owing a great deal to his mentor, Bradley Ogden, Craig explained to me that "right off the bat" he was taken to the Marin farmers' market, and "it was eye opening." Within weeks of moving to the Bay Area, he was "checking out cheesemaking and picking berries," which is what those of us in the Bay Area like to call a typical Sunday afternoon.

Warren Weber of Star Route Farms has been farming in Marin County since 1974 and is the oldest continuously certified organic grower in California. This was never Warren's plan, however. He studied agricultural economics as an undergraduate at Cornell and then became a doctoral student in the University of California–Berkeley's English department. As he was finishing his dissertation, he moved up to Bolinas as part of the "back to the land movement" and has never left.

Looking back now, he laughs about how little of his education mattered to the career path he chose. Even his coursework at Cornell was focused on production science. "The farm courses weren't about the enterprise of farming as I know it," Warren says, "they were about producing commodity crops." But in Berkeley he had a large backyard garden, and he had worked with a number of nonprofit groups dealing with land-reform issues. So he simply decided to "make a go of it."

Warren happened to start farming at the very beginning of the organic movement—the California Certified Organic Farmers had just formed in 1973—so Warren "sold to people who wanted what we were doing, which was mostly small natural food stores." Things really took off for Warren in the early 1980s when Chez Panisse forager Sibella Kraus visited and "became a good, steady account." As cooks and chefs left Chez Panisse and moved elsewhere, many would take Warren with them as a supplier, and "it just grew from there," he says.

At that time the organic industry was growing really quickly, and Warren realized he couldn't keep up with the year-round demand. In response, he expanded his acreage with twenty acres in the Coachella Valley of Southern California. "Things were looking great, business was steady, and we thought we had it all figured out . . . and then in the mid-1990s the entire organic industry changed." As larger growers saw the organic market expand, they aggressively entered the industry, and "they dropped prices and simply crushed the small growers," notes Warren. "The smaller growers needed to figure out what to do from there—us included."

He scaled back production and stopped selling to wholesalers and stores, focusing his efforts on direct sales to restaurants and farmers' markets. "All along we wanted to sell to people who really wanted our product, and we wanted to form relationships and partnerships with our customers." Today, he sells to about eighty restaurants, most of which have been around for many years.

It's the "gymnastics," as Craig calls them, that keep a business running. As Warren describes fine-tuning his business to changing markets, Craig speaks of juggling daily food quantities and irritated customers.

"If someone gets a less-than-perfect steak, they don't care about the other twenty-nine perfect steaks that left the kitchen that night." Craig likes to handle the cost point pragmatically. "Yes, we want people to eat locally from small producers, but in order to do that, they have to understand that most food is cheap in this country, and cheap food comes at a price." A price that Craig refuses to pay.

For quality produce, Craig has been buying from Star Route Farms since he was a sous chef at Splendido. "I've been involved with them forever . . . they're a special story."

Delfina's Tomato Sformatino

From Craig Stoll of Delfina

6 servings

"Sformatino" literally means "little unmolded thing" in Italian. The word refers to savory flans or soufflés (or in this case, a chilled aspic) served as a "primo" or first course. When made well, they are a direct expression of the main ingredient itself.

3 lbs. ripe tomatoes
3 cloves garlic, peeled
1 tbsp. red wine vinegar
pinch chile flake (optional)
salt
4 sheets gelatin
2 tbsp. fresh basil leaves, chopped
freshly ground black pepper
extra-virgin olive oil

First, peel and seed the tomatoes. Bring a large pot of water to a boil. Remove stems and make an *X* on the bottom of each tomato with a paring knife. Have a bowl ready with ice water for the tomatoes when they are done cooking. When the water is boiling, drop tomatoes in for about 1 minute. Remove and plunge immediately into the ice water. When cool, remove skins. Cut in half and squeeze out the seeds, reserving the juice. Strain reserved juice through a sieve to remove any remaining seeds. Using a chef's knife, mash the garlic cloves to a paste with a little salt. Puree tomatoes and the reserved juice in a blender with the garlic, vinegar, chile flake, and salt. Pass through a strainer lined with a single layer of cheesecloth. Taste and adjust the salt and vinegar if necessary. When finished, you should have 4 c. of liquid.

Soften the gelatin in cold water for about 10 minutes. When soft, squeeze dry. Heat strained tomato juice gently (do not boil) until hot, then stir in the softened gelatin until dissolved. Allow mixture to cool for about 10 minutes, then stir in the chopped basil. Pour into six disposable 4-oz. Styrofoam or plastic cups. Refrigerate overnight or until gelatin sets.

To serve, run a thin paring knife around the inside edge of the cup and unmold onto individual plates. Drizzle with extra-virgin olive oil and sprinkle with black pepper to garnish.

A few notes: We use Early Girl tomatoes or Roma tomatoes for this recipe. The recipe works well with either red or yellow varieties—the most important thing is that the tomatoes are ripe, juicy, and delicious. For the extra-virgin olive oil, we use a high-quality imported Tuscan oil. Another good oil is made by Da Vero in Sonoma.

Pappa al Pomodoro

From Craig Stoll of Delfina

6–8 servings

3 lbs. very ripe tomatoes
3 yellow onions, sliced very thin
3 cloves garlic, smashed
1 c. extra-virgin olive oil
kosher salt
black pepper
1/2 loaf crusty Italian bread
1/2 bunch basil leaves, torn

Remove the tomato cores, and, using a paring knife, score the skin on the bottom of each one with a little cross mark. Bring a pot of salted water to boil. Prepare a dish of salted ice water large enough to hold the tomatoes. Blanch the tomatoes in the boiling water for 15 seconds, then remove the tomatoes and immerse in the ice bath (this stops the cooking process). Place a strainer over a large bowl. Once cooled, peel each tomato, and, using your fingers, remove the juice and seeds from the interior pockets of the tomato. Work over the strainer, to ensure that you catch the juice and seeds. Place the tomato flesh in a separate bowl. Once all of the tomatoes have been peeled and seeded, extract as much juice as possible, then discard the seeds. Combine the tomato flesh and juice and set aside.

In a heavy-bottomed pot, add the sliced onions, well-smashed garlic, olive oil, and some salt and pepper. Put a lid on the pot and place on a burner over medium heat. Sweat the onions and garlic in the oil, stirring occasionally, until they are completely soft (no crunch) but not caramelized. Remove the crusts from half a loaf of crusty Italian bread. Tear the crustless bread into large croutons and place on a sheet tray. Toast in an oven at 275 degrees until the croutons are dried out but still the same color.

Remove the lid on the pot, add the peeled and seeded tomatoes and their juice, season with a little more salt and pepper, and simmer for approximately 15 minutes, or until tomatoes are cooked. Using a food mill, mill two-thirds of the cooked tomato-onion mixture, then add the milled tomatoes back to the pot along with the unmilled tomatoes. Return to a simmer, add the croutons, and cook for 5 minutes. Remove the soup from heat and stir in several torn basil leaves. Spoon into soup bowls, and finish with a drizzle of good extra-virgin olive oil and a twist of black pepper.

Baked Ricotta

with Zucchine Napoletana

From Craig Stoll of Delfina

1 lb. fresh ricotta

1 tsp. kosher salt

1 tbsp. vegetable oil

2–3 fig leaves

1/2 gal. peanut or rice bran oil (for frying)

1/2 c. extra-virgin olive oil

6 garlic cloves, sliced

2–3 lbs. Early Girl tomatoes or 1 can whole, peeled plum
   tomatoes

kosher salt

black pepper

2 zucchinis

fresh basil

baguette sliced into 1/2-inch-thick slices

extra-virgin olive oil

Preheat the oven to 400 degrees. Season the ricotta with the salt. Rub the inside of a small, ovenproof bowl with the vegetable oil. Line the bowl with the fig leaves, top of the leaves facing the bowl, veins to the interior. Pack the ricotta into the bowl and top with a small piece of parchment paper. Set the bowl of ricotta on a sheet tray and put in the oven. Bake for 10 minutes at 400. Lower the heat and bake for another 30 minutes at 350 degrees. When done, the ricotta should be firm but not too stiff.

In a heavy-bottomed, nonreactive saucepot, heat the olive oil. When the surface of the oil shimmers but before it smokes, add the sliced garlic. Fry the garlic until it's lightly browned and crisped. Remove the garlic from the oil onto a paper towel-lined plate. Season with kosher salt. Pass all but one of the tomatoes through a food mill to puree. Add the tomato puree to the olive oil and bring to a boil. Simmer rapidly for 15–20 minutes or until it thickens enough to coat the back of a spoon. Remove the garlic cloves and season with salt and pepper. Set aside to cool.

Slice the zucchini into very thin rounds using a mandolin. Heat the peanut oil to 350 degrees and fry the zucchini in batches until lightly browned and crisped. Transfer to a paper-towel-lined platter and season each batch with salt. Brush each bread slice with extra-virgin olive oil, soaking them thoroughly. Sprinkle with salt and bake on sheet pans at 350 degrees until lightly browned and crispy. Set aside.

To assemble, toss the fried zucchini with some of the tomato sauce, the garlic, and the basil. Cut the baked ricotta into wedges. Rub the bread rounds with a garlic clove and then with a halved tomato, grinding the tomato pulp into the toast. Arrange the ricotta with the zucchini and crostini on a platter or on individual plates.

Mission Beach Café

Owner Bill Clarke and Chef Trevor Ogden (pictured)
Far West Fungi

Bill Clarke never thought he'd be a restaurateur. He was a furniture designer for over twenty years. In 2002, he bought a building in the San Francisco Mission District that he used as a furniture design and sales space, at first. "Quite honestly, I got kind of tired of the furniture clientele I had to sell to and had to figure out what to do with the space."

In 2007, Bill turned his furniture studio into Mission Beach Café because he "wanted to do something where he could give back to the neighborhood," and the best way he could think to do that was to create "a quintessential neighborhood café."

Mission Beach Café is well known for its clever cross-cultural combinations, its full line of pastries, and its BBQ Tuesdays, which feature smoked and grilled tofu. Chef Trevor Ogden admits that he's always trying to create flavors so "there's something behind the first bite." For example, combining the simplicity of Japanese sensations with the complicated and spice-driven sauces of the French. The result? Northern California cuisine, in Trevor's eyes. "Fundamentally, it is the produce that really informs this style of food. The California style has really morphed because of the products that are available."

For Bill, the challenge is to maintain consistency and quality while setting an ambitious pattern for the small forty-two-seat café. Because of Bill's background in furniture design, he also designed the interior, including all the tables and chairs. "It's all custom done . . . to me the aesthetics are 45 percent of any meal." In fact, he readily admits that he probably spent more money on his restaurant's interior than any sane restaurateur would do. Wooden tabletops line crème-colored bench seats and chairs, all majestically balanced by exposed ceiling beams. I believe Bill is right: When you walk by the windows and peek into the cozy café space, you can't help but want to sit down for a bite, and marvel at the clever food creations.

The menu changes on a weekly basis, not necessarily dramatically, but with every seasonal shift of vegetables. "Our regular customers," Bill says, "always know what the seasons are by coming into our restaurant and looking at the menu!"

Additionally, "we're trying to keep it local and make a family outside of the restaurant with the purveyors we buy from," Bill says. For this reason, they love getting their exotic mushrooms from Far West Fungi.

Far West Fungi, owned by John and Toby Garrone, began in the Hunter's Point shipyard. John was working for the police department at the time and realized that there was empty warehouse space that could be used to grow mushrooms. "I began this routine," he said, "of dispatching police cars at night and selling and growing mushrooms by day." Ten years later he had a thriving mushroom business.

By 1990, the company had gone through several changes, and demand had grown to a point where they needed more space. As

luck would have it, they found an old mushroom-growing facility in Moss Landing that was perfect for the exotic fungi they had learned to grow.

Walking around John Garrone's plot of land, which is covered with large white warehouses, I speak to him about the lack of local mushroom farms and why that came to be. "Twenty years ago," he tells me, "shitakes had just started; we tied the price of shitakes to the price of meat in the late 1980s. When the Chinese started to import their own mushrooms, they lowered the prices, and that changed the way people thought of shitakes. It lowered their value. So a lot of people who were really involved . . . many of them fell out of the business."

Luckily for John, Far West Fungi was dealing at a farmers' market level, which enabled them to keep more of the profit than they could selling wholesale. In addition, the budding markets allowed them to introduce different types of mushrooms. But to make it profitable, they have to produce mushrooms that are able to grow in similar climates, which of course, has meant a lot of trial and error over the years. The chefs, however, don't seem to mind.

"We have a whole group of restaurants that come to the store. Many of the chefs have been coming to us for over twenty years." His customers are also well aware of the company's compliance with organic standards. The care and time involved in the mushroom's growth means a better-tasting and truer product in the long run.

This is especially important to Trevor over at Mission Beach Café. "I grew up in Chicago. Over there, the restaurant scene is about changing the food into what it's not, and I really wanted to work more directly with what the real food was."

"But hey," he adds, "I was also working down in Savannah for two and a half years doing soul food. So, you know, alligator might be next on the menu."

Pappardelle Pasta
with Morels and Mascarpone

From Trevor Ogden of Mission Beach Café

6 servings

1/2 c. extra-virgin olive oil
8 shallots, sliced
10 cloves garlic, peeled and sliced
16 spears asparagus (1/4-inch bias cut)
1/3 lb. morels, cleaned and sliced in half
6 tbsp. white wine
2 tbsp. lemon juice
6 c. mushroom stock
3/4 c. mascarpone cheese
24 oz. fresh pappardelle pasta
12 sun-dried tomatoes, sliced
1 bunch fresh marjoram
1/3 c. toasted pine nuts
grated Parmesan cheese

In an 8-qt. saucepan add the extra-virgin olive oil and turn on medium heat. When the oil gets hot but not smoking, add the sliced shallot and garlic and sweat for about two minutes, or until aroumatic. Add the asparagus and morels to the pan and continue to cook for another 2 minutes. Deglaze the pan with white wine and lemon juice, then add the mushroom stock and mascarpone cheese. Simmer the mixture for about ten minutes until the sauce coats the back of a spoon.

Meanwhile cook your pasta in seasoned boiling water until al dente. Reserve 1/4 c. of your pasta water and add to the sauce mixture with the cooked pasta. Return the pan to a low heat and add the sliced sun-dried tomatoes and fresh marjoram. Season with salt and pepper. Place into a serving dish and garnish with toasted pine nuts and freshly grated Parmesan cheese.

Mushroom Benedict

From Trevor Ogden of Mission Beach Café

8 servings

6 qts. water
2 tbsp. salt
1/2 c. white wine vinegar
16 eggs
3 tbsp. unsalted butter
6 onions, julienned
1 tsp. salt
4 tbsp. vegetable oil
1/2 lb. oyster mushrooms, cleaned
pepper
4 tbsp. butter
4 tbsp. flour
2 c. half-and-half
2 tbsp. white truffle oil
1/2 c. white cheddar cheese
8 English muffins, halved
2 c. fresh baby spinach
1 white truffle (optional)

For the poached eggs: Bring the water, salt, and vinegar to a low boil. Crack the eggs individually into a small bowl, to make sure there are no shell pieces or broken yolks, and then gently drop one by one into poaching liquid. Cook for approximitly 3 minutes for an overeasy egg. Using a slotted spoon, pull the eggs out in order of putting them in for even cooking times. Either serve right away or store in water at room tempurature for about ten minutes.

Place the 3 tbsp. of butter in a 4-qt. saucepan and melt on medium heat. Add the onions as soon as the butter is melted. Season the onions with 1 tsp. of salt and let cook while stirring frequently to prevent the onions from burning. Continue to cook until the onions are soft and caramel in color. Remove from the heat.

Add the vegetable oil to a 12-inch sauté pan and turn on high. Once the oil is hot but not smoking, add the oyster mushrooms and fry for 1 minute without stirring. Then, stir the mushrooms, season with salt and pepper, and cook for an additional 2 minutes. Strain off any excess liquid and set aside.

For the mornay sauce: In a saucepan, cook the butter and flour on low heat to create a roux. It needs to be cooked until it smells a little bit nutty, with no smell of raw flour. It should be a light caramel color. Once the roux is cooked, whisk in your half-and-half until you get a smooth consistency. Add the white truffle oil and cheese. Season with salt and store in a double boiler or thermos, which will keep it warm for an hour or so.

To assemble your benedict, start by toasting your English muffins. On each muffin place 3 tbsp. of caramelized onions, about fifteen leaves of spinach, and 3 tbsp. of oyster mushrooms. Return these to a 350 degree oven and bake for about 10 minutes. Pull out of oven and place on serving dishes. Place one poached egg on each muffin and drizzle with mornay sauce. Shave white truffle on top.

Porcini-Crusted Filet Mignon

From Trevor Ogden of Mission Beach Café

6 servings

3 tbsp. vegetable oil
3/4 c. sunchoke, peeled and sliced
3/4 c. vegetable stock
1/4 c. heavy cream
6 5-oz. filet mignon steaks
salt
pepper
1 tbsp. porcini powder
4 c. beef stock
6 tbsp. vegetable oil, divided
3 baby leeks, julienned
8 King Trumpet mushrooms, quartered
3 small porcini, sliced
1/2 c. artichoke hearts
2 tbsp. butter

For the sunchoke puree, get a sauté pan really hot, then add your oil. Right before it starts smoking, toss in the peeled sunchokes. Caramelize for 3 minutes, continuously stirring. Add your vegetable stock and heavy cream, reduce heat to a low simmer, and cook until sunchokes are tender. Place all ingredients in a blender. Blend until smooth and season with salt only. Hold in a saucepan with plastic wrap directly on top of the surface, otherwise a skin will form and make the sauce lumpy.

Season the steaks with salt and pepper, then dust with the porcini powder. Let sit at room temperature for 10 minutes. Heat a cast-iron pan until hot. Add 4 tbsp. of vegetable oil to the pan. Once the oil is smoking, add the steaks and sear until browned on all sides. Check the internal temperature with a thermometer—for medium rare, you want an internal temperature of 140 degrees. Once that temperature is reached, rest the steaks on a wire rack. Cover the steaks with aluminum foil to keep them warm. Keep all of the *fond* (residue) in the pan and add your beef stock. Reduce the heat to medium and reduce the liquid by half.

While you're waiting for the sauce to reduce, heat 2 tbsp. of vegetable oil in a separate pan. Add the julienned leeks, sweat for one minute, then add all of the mushrooms. Caramelize for a few minutes, then add the artichoke. Season the vegetable mixture with salt and pepper. Turn the reduced beef stock down to low and whisk in the butter to thicken the sauce. It is now ready to serve.

To serve, spoon some of the sunchoke puree onto each plate. Place the vegetables over that, then place your steaks on top. Drizzle with the steak pan sauce.

Mission Pie

Chefs Karen Heisler (pictured) and Krystin Rubin
Blue House Farm

The relationship that binds San Francisco's Mission Pie café with Pescadero's Blue House Farm is one central to the premise of this book. They have created a true working relationship where the chefs and farmers must work together to create two separate, sustainable, and profitable businesses bound together by one humble plant: rhubarb.

But let's not get ahead of ourselves. We must begin with the Mission Pie mantra: "Coffee and pie for five bucks." Owners Karen Heisler and Krystin Rubin believe that the idea of an eight-dollar slice of pie is absurd, and they're not afraid to say so. While ordering a seasonal pie at the counter (perhaps a sweet cherry custard, or maybe a pear frangipane tart), one would do well to notice the hand-scrawled white board located to your right.

The board is titled: "Why Don't We Make Blueberry Pie?" In a nutshell: California soil needs a lot of modification to grow blueberries; therefore, most blueberries are grown in Maine. To grow blueberries locally, the farmers charge more for their special crop, which means Mission Pie would have to charge $8 for a slice of blueberry pie. "Ten bucks for a slice plus a c. of coffee? Nah," the board concludes.

"That's also why we have walnut pie instead of pecan pie. Because in California we can grow walnuts, and pecans can only be grown in the Southeast," says Karen. During our discussion leaning against the gleaming silver worktables, Krystin points out that their commitment to environmental sustainability goes beyond just the ingredients and everyday conservation practices. In fact, she sees the limits of the restaurant's offerings as a kind of celebration.

"Those limits allow us to communicate what we're about," adds Karen, who started Mission Pie to create an environment in the city that would be able to tell stories about good food. Beyond that, she hoped to create an urban link to the community of farmers who allow Mission Pie to exist. "Without the amazing produce coming through our doors, we wouldn't be here."

At first, most people assume that only nonprofits have these sorts of visions and community ties, and many are surprised to find out that Mission Pie's progressive, for-profit business is community-oriented and successful. And this success is why Krystin began needing more rhubarb for her pies. However, even though rhubarb has an affinity for California's native soil, she could find no one locally who grew it. So she asked Ned Conwell and Ryan Casey, co-owners of Blue House Farm, to start.

Ned and Ryan have been organic farming, gardening, and teaching nature studies for over ten years. Their relationship with Mission Pie formed from a common vision of how the food system should work, and from a desire to bring small organic farms back to the West Coast. After Krystin proposed growing rhubarb locally, Ned and Ryan conducted diligent research into the growth cycle and costs of rhubarb farming. They soon realized that although California's conditions were ideal, it would take two to three years for the rhubarb to be ready for harvest, and in the meantime, they would be out a significant amount of money—more money than they had.

If the owners of Mission Pie were going to stick to their values and use locally grown foods, they would have to come up with a plan. The solution? Invest in the up-front costs of planting and growing the rhubarb, with a long-term return of locally sourced produce that otherwise wouldn't have been available.

"So how did Blue House Farm come about in the first place?" I asked. "Well, we were next-door neighbors growing up in Bonita, near San Diego," Ned and Ryan replied. In fact, they were childhood friends who, post-college, ended up having really similar experiences. Ned studied ecology and environmental education, taught at various schools, was assistant manager at Volcan View Farm and Homestead, worked at Full Belly and Mountain Bounty farms, and became an instructor for the Regenerative Design Institute. Ryan, meanwhile, taught environmental education for kids in Rhode Island, managed a mixed livestock/organic vegetable farm, traveled to New Zealand to work on various farms, and became editorial garden coordinator for *Sunset* magazine.

It was complete luck that they were able to obtain the parcel located along a beautiful stretch of San Mateo Coast, which they lease from the Peninsula Open Space Trust. "This land had probably never seen a vegetable," Ned says with a laugh. Blue House Farm started off with a tiny CSA program of about forty subscriptions for the end of the first year and slowly grew from there. Now, it is not interest in their produce that keeps them small—it is access to land, and more importantly water. "Water is one of the biggest limits to our growth," says Ryan. "It's a balance of life . . . and other people are catching on too. There are now seven small farms between Half Moon Bay and Santa Cruz, and when we started there were only two."

And of those seven, only one is growing rhubarb.

Strawberry Rhubarb Pie

From Karen Heisler and Krystin Rubin of Mission Pie

Makes 1 9-inch pie

Rhubarb, a vibrant red relative of rye, is typically available in spring. Traditionally, rhubarb has been paired with early-season strawberries that are only available in limited quantity and lend a necessary sweetness to an otherwise overly tart pie. If you like a sweeter pie, add a scant amount more sugar to this recipe.

1 3/4 c. flour
3/4 c. whole wheat flour
1 1/2 tsp. salt
1/4 tsp. baking powder
5 oz. (10 tbsp.) diced butter, cold
1/2–1 c. water, cold
1 1/2 tsp. apple cider vinegar
3 1/2 c. sliced rhubarb
2 c. strawberries, hulled
2 tsp. orange juice
1/2 c. sugar
5 tsp. tapioca starch
pinch salt
1 egg white, beaten
1/2 tsp. water
sugar, for sprinkling

In a medium bowl, combine flours, salt, and baking powder. Mix well. Using two blunt knives or a pastry blender, cut in the butter until the butter is the size of small peas. In a circular motion, quickly pour in the water and vinegar. Stir until the dough is shaggy. Grab a handful of the dough like you're shaking someone's hand. The dough should clump together when pressed. If it doesn't, add a little more water and mix more. Turn the dough out onto a lightly floured surface. Divide the dough in half, forming two disks. Wrap both disks in aluminum foil. Refrigerate for 30 minutes.

On a lightly floured surface, roll out the disks to circles with 11–12-inch diameters. Press one circle into a 9-inch pie plate. Transfer the other circle to a lightly floured board. Refrigerate both for 30 minutes. Set the oven to 450 degrees.

In a large bowl, combine the rhubarb, strawberries, orange juice, sugar, tapioca starch, and pinch of salt. Stir to combine. Pour the rhubarb mixture into the dough-lined pan. Cut a small circle in the center of the top dough. Place the top dough on the pie plate. Trim off any excess dough, leaving behind a lip of less than 1/2 inch. Press together the edge of the top and bottom dough. Using your thumb and two fingers, crimp the edges.

In a small bowl, combine the egg white and 1/2 tsp. of water. Using a pastry brush, brush the top crust with the egg wash. Sprinkle with sugar. Set the pie on a rimmed baking sheet. Place the entire thing on the bottom rack of the oven. Bake for 20 minutes. Lower the oven temperature to 400 degrees, then rotate the pie from front to back. Bake for 30 minutes longer, or until the filling is bubbling. If the crust is browning too quickly, cover the top and/or edges with aluminum foil. Remove the pie from the oven and cool on a metal cooling rack.

Swiss Chard Pie

From Karen Heisler and Krystin Rubin of Mission Pie

Makes 1 9-inch pie and an extra pie shell

Pie dough freezes exceptionally well. This recipe yields enough dough to make two crusts. If you freeze the dough as a disk, wrap it tightly in plastic and keep frozen for up to one month. Or you may choose to line a pie plate with the dough and then freeze it; store unwrapped for up to one week.

1 3/4 c. flour
3/4 c. whole wheat flour
1 1/2 tsp. salt
1/4 tsp. baking powder
5 oz. (10 tbsp.) diced butter, cold
1/2–1 c. water, cold
1 1/2 tsp. apple cider vinegar
1 bunch Swiss chard, leaves and stems separated
1 tbsp. vegetable oil
1 large onion, finely chopped
2 cloves garlic, finely chopped
4 eggs
salt and black pepper
1/4 tsp. ground nutmeg
1/2 c. Parmesan cheese

In a medium bowl, combine flours, salt, and baking powder. Mix well. Using two blunt knives or a pastry blender, cut in the butter until the butter is the size of small peas. In a circular motion, quickly pour in water and vinegar. Stir until the dough is shaggy. Grab a handful of the dough like you're shaking someone's hand. The dough should clump together when pressed. If it doesn't, add more water and mix more. Turn the dough out onto a lightly floured surface. Divide the dough in half, forming two disks. Wrap both disks in aluminum foil. Freeze one disk for another pie. Refrigerate the other disk for 30 minutes.

On a lightly floured surface, roll out a disk to a circle with a 12-inch diameter. Press the dough into a 9-inch pie plate, crimping the edges. Refrigerate for 30 minutes. Set the oven to 375 degrees. Line the pie shell with foil, pressing it firmly into the edges of the shell. Fill with baking beans. Bake the shell for 25 minutes, or until the base is pale golden. Set it aside to cool; lift out the foil and beans. Turn the oven down to 350 degrees. Let the shell cool.

Coarsely chop the Swiss chard leaves and set aside; finely chop the stems. In a large skillet over medium heat, cook the chard leaves, stirring constantly, until they wilt. Turn up the heat and cook, stirring, until the excess liquid in the pan evaporates. Transfer the leaves to a plate. Add the oil to the pan. When it is hot, add the onion, garlic, and chard stems. Cover and cook over low heat, stirring occasionally, for 8 minutes or until stems and onions are tender. Stir in the chard leaves. Transfer to the pie shell. Set the shell on a rimmed baking sheet.

In a large bowl, beat the eggs, salt, pepper, nutmeg, and Parmesan. Pour into the shell. With a fork, gently press the chard mixture into the egg mixture. Bake for 30 minutes or until the custard is just set in the center.

Piccino Café

Chefs Sher Rogat and Margherita Stewart Sagan
County Line Harvest

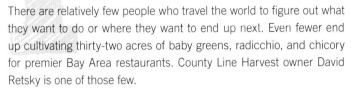

There are relatively few people who travel the world to figure out what they want to do or where they want to end up next. Even fewer end up cultivating thirty-two acres of baby greens, radicchio, and chicory for premier Bay Area restaurants. County Line Harvest owner David Retsky is one of those few.

A Los Angeles native, David first became interested in agriculture during his late years in high school, although, as most teenagers can tell you, there were so many distractions during that stage in his life . . . especially in L.A.

David admits, "There was no connection in high school to where our food comes from." So, after graduation, he spent time in Israel, Portugal, England, and Hawaii working on small farms, trying to find his place in life.

"It was my time in Israel," he recalls, "that was the beginning of my path to finding community in relation to where food comes from." These experiences left him with what keeps him motivated today: the burning desire to get back to "where our food comes from."

During my interview with Sher Rogat and Margherita Stewart Sagan from Piccino Café, it quickly becomes clear that their relationship with David revolves around their shared passion for fresh food.

"The value of growing and eating your own food is absolutely where the future of the planet is," Margherita insists. "When I read articles about how it's getting harder and harder to feed the entire population of people, I think, it's not true! Everybody just has to know how to grow a few things to be able to sustain their families." She tells me about something she heard on the radio that morning: Most Americans don't know how to cook for themselves.

"This is inconceivable for me!" she says earnestly as the look on her face changes. "It's like saying, 'You don't know how to walk?' 'You can't talk?' 'You're not able to feed yourself?'" Margherita gets upset about how we live in a monoculture where everyone brings home food that is already packaged and cooked, with no connection whatsoever to the land. This same issue made David want to farm for a living.

When Margherita first moved to the Bay Area twenty-eight years ago, she started an Italian import business. "The dire condition of what was available here was unbearable to me. I brought in whatever I could. I pioneered the sun-dried tomato. Before this, nobody even knew what they were!"

In December 2006, Margherita and Sher opened up Piccino with the help of their husbands. They started out with four employees, including themselves. Four years later, there are sixteen. I turn to Sher and ask her about what fuels her day-to-day endeavors.

"Everything that I think about with Piccino includes growing organic food. All the farmers we deal with are farmers with whom Margherita and I have had relationships prior to Piccino. It's been a joy to have them deliver directly to us, or for us to cherry-pick our food from the farmers' market and then to come back and educate our customers."

At Piccino it's not uncommon to hear a customer ask, "What is a Crescenza cheese?" or "What are Spigarello greens?" Only at a small, intimate restaurant like this would you get a response with details like where it's from, what food group it's in, and so on. Though the ingredients may sound intimidating, Margherita and Sher assure me that they are not, and their customers are not afraid to go home and try the recipes themselves.

"Our foods are so simple," says Margherita, "we go by this sort of rough rule that if there are more than five ingredients, we won't make it."

"Yeah, it's too complicated for us," Sher laughs with a dismissive wave of her hand. In addition to that, if a customer asks for extras, particularly items that are not seasonal, Sher isn't afraid to tell them "no." "When people ask us if they can have fresh tomato in the middle of winter or basil on their pizza when it's out of season, we'll tell them 'sorry, it's not in season . . . but you can have fresh oregano instead!'" Sher says, "But when it's so sincerely from the heart, people respond to that."

This dedication exemplifies how more and more restaurants are making every effort to work directly with the limited array of seasonal ingredients local farmers may be able to provide. And David with County Line Harvest appreciates this tremendously. "Part of the issue with farmers' markets is that there's much repeat in the product available. When it's tomato season, all the local farmers have tomatoes, and that makes it harder for us to sell them." Working consistently and directly with specific restaurants allows County Line to grow more freely. In addition, David tells me about how he participates in Rogue Markets—where he distributes pre-ordered "mystery boxes" of produce harvested earlier that day. "We're extremely hopeful about this concept because it's really a new distribution avenue for farm-fresh produce."

Chickpea Spread

From Sher Rogat and Margherita Stewart Sagan of Piccino Café

1 c. dried garbanzo beans
1 tbsp. salt
dash olive oil
1/2 head garlic
1/4 c. olive oil
1 lemon, juiced
salt and black pepper

Place 1 c. of dried garbanzo beans in a pot of cold water. Cover the beans completely with the water. Add the salt and olive oil. Bring to a boil and let simmer for 45 minutes. The beans should be completely cooked. Let them cool completely.

In the meantime, roast the garlic, covered in the olive oil, in an oven at 375 degrees. Take out and let cool. Take the beans and the garlic and place in a food processor. Add 1/4 c. of olive oil and the juice of one lemon. Process to a smooth puree. Salt and pepper to taste. It may need a bit more olive oil if too thick.

Lemon Tart

From Sher Rogat and Margherita Stewart Sagan of Piccino Café

6 servings

For this recipe use your favorite homemade crust or frozen puff pastry, rolled in an 8-inch tart pan.

LEMON FILLING:
1 c. sugar
2 eggs
8 tbsp. of butter, melted and cooled
juice and minced zest of 2 lemons

Preheat the oven to 375 degrees. In a food processor, place the sugar and eggs together and mix to a pale yellow. Gradually add the melted butter to the mix. Add the zest and the juice and pulse for a few more seconds. Pour the lemon filling in the tart and bake for 30 minutes.

Range

Chef Phil West and Pastry Chef Michelle Polzine
Blossom Bluff Orchards

"I like to buy from farms where I like the farmers," says Chef-Owner Phil West of Range Restaurant, "and because of that we develop a real responsibility to the food producers we work with." Chef Phil, Pastry Chef Michelle Polzine, and I sit at a cozy booth in the back of the intimate seventy-seat restaurant one winter morning discussing why they choose to work with local ingredients.

"Sometimes it can be difficult," Phil says, "because there's this mutual understanding we have with the farmers that we both have to make money, so there can be some occasional conflict there, but the personal aspect is what makes it all work for me. Buying locally is at the heart of being able to change our menu every single day as we do," he adds.

When Phil and his wife, Cameron, opened Range in 2005, they just "wanted to make food that we loved. Our vision was to make comfortable food in a comfortable setting."

Phil, who's originally from New York City, started cooking professionally in Chicago after college. He decided to enroll in Kendall College for culinary school and later moved to New Orleans to work for a year before moving to San Francisco in 1996. Though he worked at EOS and Bacar in San Francisco, Range is the first restaurant Phil has owned. I look around at the seventy-five-seat restaurant, with its self-proclaimed "pastry nook" and menu items like "marinated yellow candy onions and black trumpet mushrooms with poached farm egg, sunchoke purée, and sage," and wonder how they can do it all at such a low price point.

Phil doesn't understand why most restaurants can't perform on all fronts. When Range opened, Phil says he made a commitment to not be the type of restaurant where people love the food but complain about the bar or the service. At Range, Phil's goal is to produce high-quality food that people want, which can help support all the other bells and whistles, pretention free.

Pastry Chef Michelle Polzine came to Range from North Carolina, where the farm-to-table movement was "huge and trendy," she says; but she still came across some notions she found strange. Michelle recalls a cook she worked with who once exclaimed, "Nothing excites people more than fruit out of season!" Michelle was relieved to find that when she moved to San Francisco, people thought that notion was all wrong. The local food movement "was more entrenched and people just did it without making such a fuss over everything." She goes on to say, "If you don't cook seasonally or buy locally around here, you're kind of a jerk. You'd have to try hard not to!" In addition, says Michelle, the fun is to find exceptional ingredients she can use to make simple but special deserts. "When you pay attention to each detail, the ordinary can become extraordinary."

The Loewen family's Blossom Bluff Orchards produces some of those exceptional ingredients. Run by Ted and his wife, Fran, along

with their son, Bryce, and daughter, Renata, Blossom Bluff has been a true family affair since the 1930s, specializing in all varieties of stone fruit. The farm can be found near the San Joaquin valley town of Parlier.

Fran's grandparents, Daniel and Babette Lichti, were farm laborers in the 1920s. Through the generosity of members of their Mennonite church, they were able to buy their farm in 1931, and they lived in the same house that Ted and Fran still dwell in. The farm was passed to Fran's father, Herb Lichti, who "farmed that land from when he was in high school all the way until he was in his eighties," Fran remembers.

Fran met Ted in college, and they "never dreamed of becoming farmers." After college Ted studied law at UC Hastings College of Law and later practiced law in Fresno. After Bryce and Renata were born, Fran started working as a teacher.

Ted had stopped lawyering at that point and was working for a nonprofit. He was also becoming increasingly interested in the family business. Then Fran's father quit farming, and they realized the importance of keeping the farm in the family. "No one else wanted to take over the farm," Fran said, "and so we started taking on an increasing role to allow our parents to stay."

The Loewens made the transition to full-time farming "about five years ago." The farm has been through other transitions as well. Before they took over there were about 20 varieties of stone fruit on the eighty acres they farmed. Now there are about 180 varieties. They also made the transition to organic farming, "which was a real rough transition for my father," Fran says, "because he was proud to always keep the farm weed free and now we were supposed to have weeds beneath our trees."

But it's okay, because this year those trees will be producing chef-favorite fruits such as chocolate persimmons, pummelos, mandarins, and even Damson plums . . . a specialty that Michelle has been waiting for.

Summer Grand Nectarine
with Jasmine Blossom Ice Cream and a Sesame Plum Cookie

From Pastry Chef Michelle Polzine

6 servings

JASMINE BLOSSOM ICE CREAM:
- 1 c. freshly picked jasmine blossoms, packed
- 1/2 c. plus 1 tbsp. sugar
- 2 1/4 c. cream
- 1 1/4 c. half-and-half
- 5 fluid oz. egg yolks, placed in a small bowl

Place the blossoms in a bowl. Pour the sugar on top. Rub the sugar into the blossoms to extract their aroma and flavor. Warm the cream and half-and-half in a nonreactive pot. Pour the warm cream over the blossom sugar. Steep until the flavor is intense, but not bitter. Strain and return the cream to the pot. Scald. Temper the mixture into the egg yolks. Return all to the pot, and cook gently, heating the mixture to 170 degrees. Strain immediately and cool over an ice bath. Chill until ready to churn. (Make the base 1 day ahead if possible. Can be made 3 days ahead.) Churn according to the ice cream machine manufacturer's instructions.

SESAME PLUM COOKIE:
- 4 oz. melted butter
- 1/3 c. sugar
- 3/4 tsp. salt
- 4 oz. very soft butter
- 2 c. all-purpose flour (gently spooned and leveled), sifted
- 1/3–1/2 c. sesame seeds
- 1/3 c. low-sugar plum jam (homemade is best)

Whisk together the melted butter, sugar, and salt. Whisk in the soft butter, followed by the flour. Divide in two, saving half for later. Scrape the other half of the dough onto a sheet of plastic wrap, covering with another sheet. Roll the dough into a rectangle about 1/8-inch thick. Chill.

Preheat the oven to 300 degrees. Slit rectangle lengthwise to form two equal elongated rectangles. (Eventually these will be sliced crosswise to form your cookie, so keep the shape you prefer in mind). Remove the plastic from one rectangle and spread the top with a layer of sesame seeds, pressing them into the dough. Flip that dough over onto a parchment-lined baking sheet, remove the top sheet of plastic, and repeat the sesame application. Repeat with the other piece of dough. (Be sure to catch wandering sesame seeds to press in.) Chill again for at least 10 minutes.

Bake until lightly golden. Spread the jam on one of the halves, and using a very large offset spatula (or two smaller ones) slide the naked half on top of the jammy half. Bake until golden; the seeds will remain light in color. With a sharp serrated knife, neatly trim and slice into cookies while still warm. Serve same day. Dough can be made, cut, and seeded in advance.

SOAKING SYRUP:
- 1/4 c. mild honey
- 1/2 c. water
- 1/2–1 c. dessert wine, such as Muscat Beaume des Venise or a late-harvest Riesling

Whisk together ingredients and set aside.

NECTARINES:
Slice three nectarines in two along their seams, twisting and removing the pits. Slice a tiny piece off the back of each one. Save little pieces, and place nectarines in a single layer, cut-side down, in a flat glass dish. Pour syrup over, flipping occasionally to marinate for 15 minutes–2 hours before serving. You may reduce a little of the syrup with the little pieces of nectarine as a plate sauce. Strain out nectarine bits before plating.

To assemble, place the nectarines on plates. Drizzle a little syrup around the plate, leaving one spot dry. Fill the cavity of each nectarine with a scoop of ice cream, and place one or two cookies on the dry spot on your plates. Place one or two blossoms on each plate to make it fancy. Serve immediately.

July Red Nectarines
with Wild Arugula, Walnuts, and Fromage Blanc

From Phil West of Range

6 servings

SALAD:

  2–3 each July Red nectarines
  1 lb. wild arugula, washed and drained
  1 large head frisee, washed and trimmed of green leaves
  salt and black pepper
  1 c. walnuts, lightly toasted
  6 oz. fromage blanc
  Champagne Vinaigrette (see recipe below)

Cut each nectarine into several wedges. In a large bowl, combine the arugula and the frisee. Season lightly with salt and pepper. Break the walnuts with your hands into the bowl—it's okay if there are odd-sized pieces. Have six salad plates ready for plating.

Lightly dress the greens, tossing gently. Add the fruit to the bowl and mix. Arrange the salad equally on the salad plates. Dot each salad with about 1 oz. of fromage blanc. Drizzle the salad with additional olive oil and a grind of black pepper.

CHAMPAGNE VINAIGRETTE:

  1 small shallot, minced fine
  2 oz. champagne vinegar
  1 tsp. Dijon mustard
  3 oz. grape seed oil
  3 oz. olive oil, plus more for drizzling
  salt and black pepper

Macerate the shallot with the vinegar. Season lightly and let stand 10–15 minutes. Whisk in mustard. Combine the oils and slowly drizzle into the shallot mixture, whisking constantly. Adjust seasoning to taste.

Slow Club

Chef Matthew Paul

Free Spirit Farm

Slow Club's Chef Matthew Paul met farmer Toby Hastings at a slow food dinner for the Center for Land-Based Learning (CLBL) in 2008. Chef Matt had just recently started working at Slow Club and was looking for more farm partners. Toby had just started leasing land from CLBL to farm and was looking for new restaurant customers. A new relationship was born.

Slow Club is "a small neighborhood restaurant that focuses on being 95 percent farm-to-table," says Matt. One reason, he admits, is that his kitchen is so small he needs to buy a little bit every day to stay supplied. But he's always been interested in what's fresh from the garden, even as a child in Michigan. Growing up, he says "We always had a garden, and I could always tell the difference between the food from the store and the food from the garden. And I didn't like tomatoes except those we picked ourselves!"

Matt went to Michigan State University to study engineering, but decided he didn't want to be in the auto industry, which is what was available to him at the time. So he came to California to attend culinary school instead.

He's proud that at Slow Club, "we've toured every farm we buy from. You can just look around and tell if the food's going to be good, if the land is natural, and if you think it's a place you'd want to eat from.

"What really impressed me about Toby's farm were all the native plants and the millions of dragonflies everywhere. And this amazing sleek-haired fox ran by, and there were native bees everywhere. It's a special place. See, look at those flowers," he points toward the kitchen. "He's growing our flowers for us as well."

Toby only started farming his two acres a few years ago, after graduating from UC Santa Cruz with a degree in geology. He returned home to Davis, where he grew up, and started looking for some land to farm. "A friend of mine was working for CLBL, and told me they were looking for someone to partner with to start a demonstration farm. So now I give tons of tours, and there are demonstrations and groups out here all the time."

The Audubon Society also helps to manage some of the surrounding land for native birds and wildlife, partnering with local schools to teach students about the interrelationships between plants, insects, birds, and other wildlife.

The land Toby grows on is certified organic, and he doesn't use any sprays, "but I am not a certified organic producer yet. I sell only direct to people who know and trust me though, so it's not a big deal for me to be certified," he said. He sells to a very small thirty-five-member CSA, ten different restaurants, and seasonally at one farmers' market in Davis.

"Restaurants give me a little less of a price point for the produce I sell," he said, "but then I don't have to worry about having ten things in

my CSA box. And if I have a huge restaurant order one week and sell out my eggplant, I just don't give that in the CSA box the next week, so it kind of works out for me."

But he does like diversity. This spring he ordered about forty different kinds of melon, just to see what would grow. I walk up to a large dark green one and ask what it is. He shakes his head, "it's cool looking, isn't it? But I don't know what it is, there are too many. I'll have to look up the ones that do well!"

Walnuts surround Toby's farm because CLBL was founded by walnut farmer Craig McNamara. Audubon and Toby share the shade-house space—Audubon growing native seedlings, and Toby growing his heirloom plants. "And I'm hoping in the future to grow mushrooms in here," he says.

Grilled Pork Loin with Fresh Shelling Beans

From Matthew Paul of Slow Club

6 servings

3 lbs. fresh shelling beans (e.g., cranberry, coco blanc, butter beans), approximately 2 lbs., shucked

1 small yellow onion, root end intact, cut in quarters

1 large carrot, roughly cut into 2-inch pieces

2 gals. cold water

salt

2 tbsp. extra-virgin olive oil

1 lb. lemon cucumber, cut into 1/2-inch cubes

2 tbsp. butter

1 lb. heirloom tomatoes, cut into 1/2-inch cubes

1 lemon, juiced

3 tbsp. parsley, chopped

3 lbs. boneless pork loin cut into 6 8-oz. portions

1/2 lb. Baby Red mustard greens

2 tbsp. extra-virgin olive oil

1 lemon, juiced

1/4 c. Red Wine Gastrique (see recipe below)

For the beans: In a large stock pot, combine the shucked beans, onion, carrot, and cold water. Over medium-high heat, bring to a simmer, then reduce heat to medium-low. Continue cooking at a low simmer for approximately 30 minutes, adding salt (about 1/4 c.). Remove from the heat and let stand in warm water until the beans are al dente. Discard the onion and carrot. Strain the beans, reserving 2 c. of cooking liquid. In a medium saucepan bring the beans, with 1 c. of cooking liquid and 2 tbsp. of olive oil, to a boil. Reduce the heat to low. Add the cucumbers. Stir in the butter to emulsify, them remove from the heat. Add the tomatoes, lemon juice, and parsley. Taste for seasoning.

For the pork: Heat a grill (or bring a fire) to medium-high heat. Season the pork, placing it on the grill directly over the fire. Cook on each side about 6–8 minutes or until desired doneness. Let rest at least 5 minutes.

For the mustard greens: In a large mixing bowl, dress the greens with olive oil and lemon juice. Season to taste.

To plate, place the bean, cucumber, and tomato mix in the center of each plate or bowl. Top with the dressed mustard greens, then the grilled pork. Drizzle the gastrique around the plate and a little on top of the pork.

RED WINE GASTRIQUE:

375 ml (1/2 bottle) dry red wine (like Cabernet Sauvignon)

1/4 c. red wine vinegar

1 c. sugar

In a small saucepan combine all the ingredients. Bring to a boil. Immediately reduce the heat to medium-low and simmer for approximately 45 minutes. Remove from the heat, cooling to room temperature. (When finished, hot gastrique should be the consistency of warm honey. Be careful not to over-reduce, as the gastrique will become bitter.)

Arugula Salad with Strawberries

From Matthew Paul of Slow Club

6 servings

1 1/2 lbs. arugula

1 pt. strawberries, sliced

Moscato Vinaigrette (see recipe below)

salt and black pepper

1 c. pecans, lightly toasted and chopped

6 oz. feta cheese, crumbled

In a large mixing bowl, combine the arugula and strawberries. Dress with Moscato Vinaigrette and season to taste.

To plate, divide the dressed arugula and strawberries between six plates, or place on one large platter. Garnish with pecans and feta cheese.

MOSCATO VINAIGRETTE:

3/4 c. Moscato vinegar (if Moscato vinegar is not available, white balsamic vinegar is fine)

1 tsp. shallots, minced

1 tsp. fresh thyme, chopped

1/2 tsp. whole-grain mustard

1 c. extra-virgin olive oil

salt and black pepper

Combine the first four ingredients in a mixing bowl. Slowly whisk in the olive oil. Season to taste.

Woodward's Garden

Chefs Dana Tommasino (pictured) and Margie Conard
Terra Sonoma

Susan Stover rests comfortably on a chair in the garden outside her house in Sonoma County. She is talking about the San Francisco restaurant Woodward's Garden, saying, "When Dana [Tommasino] calls to place an order, it just really makes my day. She always starts her order by saying 'What's beautiful today?'"

From the beginning, at the core of Woodward's were quality ingredients combined with the energy it takes to create them. Dana Tommasino, working in the kitchen of Greens restaurant, "came across the nicest produce I've ever seen." She remembers the experience of getting lettuces from Green Gulch Farm as being a revelation. The leaves had more color and richer taste than any other greens she'd seen before. It was then that she realized creating a delicious restaurant menu with only top-quality ingredients wasn't far from reach.

When they first opened Woodward's in 1992, Dana and her partner, Margie Conard, both worked in the kitchen together. Over the years, however, a natural separation has occurred where Dana runs the kitchen and Margie manages the front of the house. For Dana, this also means being in charge of the menu, which she creates from what is available each morning. "The menu is a puzzle and a game, and it suits my personality," she says. "I like the challenge of making it all work, and sometimes I don't figure it all out until I'm on my way to work that day."

Back in 1992, "it was relatively inexpensive to open a restaurant in the way that we were," Dana says. "On the edge of the Mission District, it was a really rough neighborhood, and we're tucked underneath this freeway." But enough people found this tucked-away little gem to make it a hit. "It's funny it's so popular now because it's always been our thing. And it's not just about the final product, it's about the process."

Part of that process involves where they buy their produce—from Terra Sonoma.

Around the same time that Dana and Margie opened their little restaurant in the mission, two gardeners living in San Francisco found an oasis of land about sixty-five miles to the north. Susan Stover and Tony Sadoti found an old farmhouse on ten acres of land with a fairly level lot and enough water for a garden. They thought they were looking at paradise. What they were really buying, looking back, was "a house that was crap and cars and boarded-up windows. It was a real wreck."

They started fixing it up and slowly clearing a garden and orchard space. "At first we had to take twenty loads of metal and trash out of the field, and we got it all cleaned up and started growing," Tony said. They loved gardening but didn't know what to do with all their produce, so they found a woman who lived nearby who took produce into San Francisco and Berkeley to sell. Tony thought, "We can be one of her suppliers," and they started growing for her. They grew baby squash, fennel, leeks, carrots—anything that would grow in their

climate and soil. Then, in 1994, they were asked if they wanted to buy the business.

Tony built a packing house and office, bought a big truck, and started making the deliveries. Susan took over the duties of taking the orders and getting them packed. "It's very hands-on, and Susan tries to match the right product with each chef. For example, if she knows that a chef has a preference for a certain farm's beets, she tries to keep everyone happy."

Tony describes how different their business is from a typical distributor: "Everything is picked and cut to order. We don't buy produce and then try to sell it. Everything is picked when it is bought, and so we don't waste much." And, he continues, the chefs get the freshest produce possible.

Over the years the customer base has changed, he says, "but there are still people who buy from us who were buying from our predecessor in the late 1980s, it's basically still running the way it always did." They often get new accounts when a chef they sell to leaves to start his or her own restaurant and takes Terra Sonoma on as a supplier. At the same time, Tony admits, "This business has built-in limitations. We can't supply too big of a customer base, so the inherent balance of supply and demand is maintained."

In 2005, Susan and Tony established their first three-acre orchard. They planted species that thrived in the maritime environment, including seven varieties of plums (with two types of prunes), seven kinds of pears, and two types of apples. They sell their fruit, in season, along with that of the other producers they work with.

In addition to their orchard, garden, and now beautifully restored house, they raise about forty chickens, as well as some goats and pigs. As we walk around her garden, Susan fills her basket with bunches of weeds. "I have a good deal of weeds in the garden that I'm letting go to seed for the chickens," she explains. We then walk over to the chicken shed, and she hand-feeds each chicken to make sure they are fed the right way. Whether selling to a chef or feeding an animal, she displays the same kindness and compassion.

Sautéed Goat Cheese–Stuffed Squash Blossoms with Tomatillo Salsa

From Dana Tommasino and Margie Conard of Woodward's Garden

4 servings

We get vibrant, peppery squash blossoms all summer long from Terra Sonoma. Cornmeal, tomatillos, and cilantro pull these crisped blossoms well into the Southwest. They're also wonderful simply drizzled with herb oil.

TOMATILLO SALSA:

1 lb. of tomatillos, peeled, rinsed, and dried
1 small head of garlic, cut in half widthwise
1/2 red onion, peeled and cut into 1-inch wedges
1/2 pasilla chile, seeded and cut into 1-inch strips
olive oil
sea salt and freshly ground pepper
1/4 c. water
1/4 c. picked cilantro leaves

Preheat the oven to 375 degrees. Place the tomatillos on a sheet pan. Add the garlic (cut side down), onion, and chile. Drizzle all of it with 3 tbsp. of olive oil and season with salt and pepper. Roast for 30–40 minutes until fragrant and the tomatillos start to lightly brown. Cool and puree in a blender or food processor with 1/4 c. of olive oil, the water, and the cilantro. Taste and season with more salt and pepper if necessary. Set aside.

SAUTÉED SQUASH BLOSSOMS:

1/4 c. flour
1/4 c. cornstarch
1/4 c. cornmeal
sea salt and freshly ground pepper
1/2 c. crème fraîche or sour cream
1/2 c. milk
12 medium squash blossoms
3/4 c. Cypress Grove goat cheese, or another mild, creamy
   goat cheese
1/4 c. olive or canola oil

Mix the dry ingredients in a small bowl. Mix the crème fraîche and the milk in a small bowl. Gently open the squash blossoms, snap off the interior stem, and fill with about 1 tbsp. of goat cheese; gently fold the blossoms back around the cheese. Dip the stuffed blossoms in the milk/cream mixture, shake off a little, then dip in the flour/cornmeal mixture and gently shake off again. Heat a heavy medium sauté pan over high heat and add oil. When hot add the squash blossoms and sauté over medium heat for 2–3 minutes until golden. Gently flip the blossom over and brown the other side the same way.

ASSEMBLY:

Tomatillo Salsa
about a c. of fresh, peppery greens, like arugula or watercress
Sautéed Squash Blossoms

Place a good spoonful of tomatillo salsa at the center of each plate. Nestle a handful of greens on top of the salsa and place three warm squash blossoms on top of the greens.

Roasted Figs and Wild Blackberries with Lemon Verbena Crème Anglaise

From Dana Tommasino and Margie Conard of Woodward's Garden

4 servings

The wild mingling flavors of melted figs, flower honey, native berries, and perfumed verbena make this tiny assemblage trill.

ROASTED FIGS:

1 pt. figs (10–12 figs), stem on, rinsed, dried, and cut in half lengthwise

3 tbsp. wildflower honey

salt

5 sprigs fresh thyme

Preheat the oven to 375 degrees. Place the figs cut side up in a baking dish. Drizzle with the honey and sprinkle with a pinch of salt. Tuck the thyme stems around the figs. Bake for 20–30 minutes until the figs puff up a bit and their juices start to run. Set aside.

LEMON VERBENA CRÈME ANGLAISE:

5 egg yolks

3/4 c. milk

3/4 c. cream

3 tbsp. sugar

1/2 vanilla bean, scraped, seeds saved

1 stem lemon verbena (for about 5 leaves), rinsed and hand crushed

Have your egg yolks ready in a medium metal bowl. In a medium saucepan mix the milk, cream, sugar, verbena leaves, and vanilla bean and seeds together. Bring to a scald over medium heat, then take the mixture off the heat and let the flavors infuse for about 10 minutes. Bring back to a scald over medium heat. Whisk half of the mixture into the egg yolks, then whisk it all back into the saucepan. Cook over medium heat, constantly stirring with a wooden spoon, until slightly thickened, about 5 minutes. Strain through a fine strainer and cool over an ice bath, stirring occasionally. Refrigerate if not using immediately.

ASSEMBLY:

Lemon Verbena Crème Anglaise
Roasted Figs
1/2 pt. wild blackberries
wildflower honey for drizzling (optional)

Spoon some of the verbena anglaise into a desert bowl or glass. Gently top with four or five fig halves and a drizzle of their cooking liquid. Sprinkle with wild blackberries and finish with a little drizzle of honey if desired.

Ragout of Fresh Shell Beans, Cipollinis & Chanterelles

Ragout of Fresh Shell Beans, Cipollinis, and Chanterelles
with Grilled Flat Iron and Pimenton Butter

From Dana Tommasino and Margie Conard of Woodward's Garden

4 servings

By late summer, fresh shell beans, cipollinis (wild Italian onions), and chanterelles seem to be everywhere. The grow together/go together axiom holds mighty true here. This dish is a no-brainer as far as mutual affinities go. Flat Iron is a rediscovered shoulder/muscle steak cut that is full of serious steak flavor. Spanish pimenton (smoked paprika) gives breadth to the dainty new beans and sweet, squat onions, and boosts the smoke of the apricot-y chanterelles and the charred meat. Think earthy mushroom/honey-onioned goodness.

PIMENTON BUTTER:

4 oz. of butter (1 stick), softened

1 tsp. smoked paprika

1/4 c. chives, chopped

1/4 c. tarragon or parsley, chopped

3 anchovies, mashed

1 shallot, minced

1 lemon, zest and juice

sea salt and black pepper

Cream together the butter, paprika, herbs, anchovies, and shallot. Add the lemon zest and juice. Taste and season if necessary. The butter should be pungent. Shape into a log in a piece of plastic wrap or parchment paper. Twist the ends to tighten and refrigerate until firm.

SHELL BEAN, CIPOLLINI, AND CHANTERELLE RAGOUT:

1 lb. cipollini onions

olive oil

sea salt and freshly ground black pepper

2 lbs. shell beans (for about 2 c. shelled; try cranberry, flageolet, or cannellini)

bunch of thyme

1 bay leaf

1 chile de arbol, snapped in half widthwise and seeded

1/2 lb. chanterelle mushrooms, cut into 1-inch wedges

1 large garlic clove, minced

3/4 c. chicken stock, preferably homemade

2 tbsp. butter

Preheat oven to 375 degrees. Fill a medium saucepan with water and bring to a boil. Add the cipollinis and blanch for about 1 minute. Drain, cool, and peel. Toss with 2 tbsp. of olive oil and a good pinch of salt and pepper. Spread out on a sheet pan. Bake for about 45 minutes or until golden and tender. Check and shake the pan every so often. Set aside.

Place the shelled beans in a medium saucepan and cover with 2 inches of water. Add six sprigs of thyme, the bay leaf, and the chile. Bring to a boil then simmer until tender, about 30 minutes. Drain. Pull out the herbs and chile. Toss the warm beans with 2 tbsp. of olive oil and a pinch of salt and pepper. Set aside.

Clean the chanterelles with a soft cloth or napkin. Cut into even, 1-inch wedges. (Leave them whole if they're small.) Heat 2 tbsp. of olive oil in a medium sauté pan until very hot. Add the chanterelles and cook over medium heat for about 7 minutes, stirring every so often, until tender and golden. Add the garlic, a tsp. of picked thyme, and a pinch of salt and pepper. Sauté for another minute. Add the cipollinis, the shell beans, and the stock. Cook for about 5 more minutes until creamy. Swirl in butter and taste. Season again if necessary. Set aside.

ASSEMBLY:

4 flatiron steaks, about 5 oz. each

olive oil

sea salt and freshly ground black pepper

Shell Bean, Cipollini, and Chanterelle Ragout

Pimenton Butter

1 c. arugula, or other fresh, spicy green (like watercress)

Fire up the grill. When hot, brush the steaks with olive oil and sprinkle with salt and pepper. Grill to desired doneness, about 4 minutes per side for medium rare. Remove and set on a plate, lightly covered with foil. While the steaks are resting, reheat the ragout if necessary. Place about 1/2 c. of ragout into the center of a warmed serving plate or bowl. Top with a steak and any accumulated steak jus, a round of pimenton butter, and a little handful of fresh greens.

South Bay

As you head down Highway 1 from San Francisco, the ocean brings in fog with a cool onshore breeze, creating ideal conditions for the farms that line the inland valleys. The South Bay region boasts an abundance of delicious and amazingly diverse crops that are served straight from the farms directly to you.

Flea Street Café

Chef Jesse Cool
Full Belly Farm

"I keep costs down by keeping it simple," Jesse Cool says with a shrug, "but I never compromise my principles about what I buy." As we sit in the garden behind her house, I can't help but wonder, *But really Jesse, what does simple mean to you—a restaurateur, lecturer at Stanford University, gardener, chef, author, and, yes, featured television personality?*

Jesse Cool was raised by a Jewish-Italian mother whose knack for lively and authentic food was supported wholeheartedly by her father's organic garden. Needless to say, Jesse's appreciation for food and gardening was ingrained at an early age. After working as a waitress at the Good Earth Restaurant, she decided to branch out on her own and opened her first restaurant in 1976.

"All of our food was locally sourced. . . . It was here that I learned an appreciation for clean food, pesticide-free food, and chemical-free food." However, when she first opened the Late for the Train Café in Menlo Park in the mid-1970s, she actually had to downplay the organic nature of the restaurant's food so as not to alienate her core customers. But her customers did keep coming back because the food tasted so fresh.

"It's very old fashioned, getting back to the real definition of fresh," she says. As we discuss how the idea of farm-to-table has been pushed aside for the all-too-familiar processed foods and big-name companies, she rushes to point out that "there's nothing wrong with the frozen foods, dried foods, and preserved foods, if they all come from original and honest sources." I have to agree.

"Our farmers are our heroes," she goes on to say. "It's the farmers and growers who have always taught us about how to use their food. As chefs, we struggle with the challenge that real food comes in different sizes and shapes, harvest times and delivery times, et cetera. I'm just a cook, like everyone else, and learning every day how to use the real food that comes to me from my farmers."

There are people, however, such as farmer Dru Rivers, who would hardly agree that Jesse Cool is just a cook. "I've known Jesse for a *really* long time," she told me one afternoon.

It's not surprising that these two women, with their similar demeanors and genuine smiles, would find each other within the world of food. Dru grew up, just as Jesse did, with a backyard garden and devoted parents. "I'm a New Englander—Vermont—and as you know, Vermonters are notorious gardeners, so my dad and mom had huge gardens when I was growing up." After finishing high school in Vermont, she left for California to attend the University of California–Davis as an agricultural student. While earning her degree in plant science and entomology, she became involved in the student-run farm and practiced her hand in management for a few years. "Then I met Paul, my husband, square dancing . . . and that was the beginning of Full Belly Farm."

Unlike most local, family-owned farms, Fully Belly didn't start small. It did, however, start out untamed. "We originally started farming on sixty acres in 1984 and slowly added pieces as the years went on. The land, though, had been severely neglected and not farmed for about ten years, so it was about as organic as land gets. . . . We certified it organic the first year we were here."

Around 1995, Full Belly started a CSA that has grown to 1,500 members. In fulfilling their vision, approximately 30 percent of what they grow goes to the CSA, 20 percent goes to markets, and the other 50 percent is sold wholesale and direct. Full Belly Farm is now owned by Andrew Brait, Paul Muller, Judith Redmond, and Dru Rivers, and they have the help of about fifty employees.

"We have become more and more diverse, and now grow over a hundred different things. . . . We've been really influenced by restaurants; those restaurants have often encouraged us to grow things that we would have never tried." In fact, even the wheat they now grow for flour is of an heirloom variety, a specific variety requested by one of their fifty or so restaurant customers.

"I would just say that in 1984 things were really different than they are now. Our farm was really in the right place at the right time. Where once people were excited on a small scale, the sustainable farming movement has now hit the masses, and for Full Belly, the ride has been fun. We have a lot of educational programs, and we have school groups visiting every week, and in the summer we have summer camps. We all really wanted to have all kinds of people experience the farm as we were. The more people that have seen and touched your farm, the more they become really invested in what you're doing."

Baby Beets
with Goat Cheese
and Pistachios

Baby Beets with Goat Cheese and Pistachios

From Carlos Canada of Flea Street Café

4 servings

Carlos Canada, chef de cuisine of Flea Street Café, has brought great inspiration to the farm-to-table philosophy that has for decades been a part of our restaurants and catering operations. His use of simple ingredients, paired well, can be both beautiful and delicious, as exemplified in this lovely salad.

3 medium beets (gold, red, or white, or chioggas)
1/2 c. olive oil, divided
1 medium shallot, minced fine
1–2 tbsp. fresh oregano, chopped fine
1 tbsp. fresh thyme, chopped fine
1 tbsp. capers
3 tbsp. red wine vinegar
1/2 tsp. Dijon mustard
1 medium orange
1 medium fennel
6 oz. arugula
salt and black pepper
1/4 c. pistachios
3 oz. goat cheese

Preheat oven to 400 degrees. Scrub the beets. Toss the beets in 2 tbsp. of the olive oil, season with salt and pepper, and place in a small roasting pan. Cover the pan with foil. Roast for about 35 minutes or until tender when pierced with the tip of a sharp knife. Remove from the oven and cool to where they can be handled.

In a small bowl, combine the remaining olive oil, shallot, oregano, thyme, capers, vinegar, and mustard. Season with salt and pepper and set aside at room temperature. Peel and cut the orange into segments. (You can peel the segments or not.) Slice the fennel as thin as possible.

In a medium bowl, toss the beets, orange segments, fennel, and arugula with the dressing and season with salt and pepper. Divide onto four plates or one large platter and garnish with pistachios and goat cheese.

Baked Tomatoes Stuffed with Sweet Corn and Dungeness Crab

From Jesse Cool of Flea Street Café

6 servings

Serve these tomatoes as a luscious summery lunch, room temperature with crusty bread and a green salad. If you don't have access to crab, substitute any cooked white-fleshed fish or canned tuna.

6 medium ripe tomatoes
**1 c. fresh corn kernels, blanched in boiling water for 1 minute,
  then cooled**
1 1/2 c. fresh crabmeat
1/2 tsp. chopped jalapeno pepper
3 tbsp. green onion, chopped
1 tbsp. fresh tarragon, chopped
1/2 tsp. lemon zest
1/4–1/3 c. mayonnaise
salt and black pepper
extra chopped onions to garnish

With a sharp knife, remove the tops of the tomatoes, and cut an opening large enough to scoop out the seeds and as much of the juicy inner flesh as possible. Be sure to leave at least 1/4–1/2 inch of flesh around the exterior of the tomato to hold the crab filling. Turn tomatoes upside down to drain while preparing the filling.

In a medium bowl, combine the corn, crabmeat, jalapeno, green onion, lemon zest, and enough mayonnaise to moisten. Season with salt and pepper. Turn the tomatoes over and lightly salt and pepper the interior. Fill each tomato with crab filling. Top each with the remaining chopped onions.

Grilled Salmon on Chive Blossom Mashed Potatoes

From Jesse Cool of Flea Street Café

4 servings

If you can't get wild salmon, use any flaky moist fish that grills well. I especially like this dish with mashed purple potatoes, or in the dead of winter substitute yams. For a lighter version of mashed potatoes, use buttermilk instead of sour cream. If you can't find chive blossoms, used chopped chives.

- 1/2 c. crème fraîche or sour cream
- 1/3 c. cucumber, peeled and grated
- 2 tbsp. red onion, grated
- 1 tbsp. dry vermouth (optional)
- salt and freshly ground black pepper
- 2 lbs. potatoes (red, golden, or purple)
- 3–4 tbsp. unsalted butter
- 6 generous tbsp. sour cream
- milk to thin
- 3–4 tbsp. chive blossoms
- 1 1/2–2 lbs. salmon
- 2 tbsp. olive oil

Prepare your outdoor grill for the fish. Bring a pot of water to boil. Meanwhile, in a small bowl, combine the crème fraîche, cucumber, red onion, vermouth, and salt and pepper. Set aside until ready to use.

Peel the potatoes and cut into even pieces. Boil in a pot until tender when tested with a fork. Drain the potatoes and put them through a ricer, or mash with a mixer or by hand. Add the butter, sour cream, and milk to desired consistency. Add the chive blossoms, reserving some for garnishing. Season with salt and pepper.

Pour some olive oil into a bowl and coat the fish. Season with salt and pepper. Grill the fish to medium rare. Remove from the grill and serve on top of a mound of the mashed potatoes. Top with crème fraîche and cucumber mixture, and garnish with extra blossoms.

Martin's West

Chef Michael Dotson

La Luna Farms

"Here in America, you call it 'farm-to-table,'" but in Scotland," Moira Beveridge informs me, "the saying is 'nature-to-plate.'" Where can you find this Scottish "nature-to-plate" cooking in California? At a gastropub called Martin's West. Moira opened Martin's West with Chef Michael Dotson to serve up Scottish-inspired but locally sourced fare. Chef Michael says, "We're still learning a little bit about how to work the menu because we realized that a strictly English menu was foreign to American consumers." As a result, they've "simplified the terminology, and that helped make it more approachable," but sustainability is still key. Indeed, as their website points out, "Sustainability is nothing new to the Scots—they were always thrifty about food as they utilized all parts of the animal (haggis, anyone?)."

Michael started cooking in Santa Barbara. As he describes it, he was on a "sort of quest to find something creative to do." Growing up in San Marcos, just east of Carlsbad, California, he was basically a fun-loving surfer who started attending art classes. He and a buddy once received an assignment to bring in a 3x5-foot painting they had made. Instead, to "push the envelope, we built an eight-foot tall sculpture and hung a 3x5 frame on it! The teacher didn't know what to do with us!" His jovial, can-do attitude is addictive and shines through in his food.

He never went to culinary school, but working in Santa Barbara—where mountain bikers would bring wild mushrooms to the back doors of restaurants to sell—he learned the importance, and cost effectiveness, of buying locally. When he made his way to San Francisco, he was surprised to find that there were few people sourcing locally. Slowly but surely, he was able to "get back into it as farmers started to become easier to find and began growing more things for restaurants." Soon after he noticed other people "moving back in that direction as well."

The funny thing is, although "farm-to-table" quite adequately describes Michael's culinary preference, he says, "I don't like the term 'farm-to-table' because it labels it, and it's just the way you should be buying."

Always looking for new small farmers producing excellent products, he heard about Mark Biaggi of La Luna Farms from a chef friend of his. I drove up to see Mark and his farm in Manchester, California, on a beautiful weekend afternoon. My family tagged along, and we were introduced to his flock of sheep and drove of swine. "They're friendly," he assured me with a smile as four half-ton pigs came galloping toward us, "so long as you don't have any open toes showing."

Mark's family has been ranching and dairy farming on this very piece of coastline since 1911. Mark went to the University of California–Davis to study agricultural science and economics. While there, he remembers how he "almost stopped eating meat, and did quit drinking milk, as they were so bad at the university dining hall compared to what I grew up on. At that time, I didn't comprehend

grass-based meat and raw milk versus standard American food, but my unsophisticated taste buds did."

After college he went into the Peace Corps in Guatemala and saw firsthand how "they didn't even know the basics they should have known about animal husbandry. The animals were starving." It was something that struck a chord in him, and he realized even he had a lot to learn about how to raise animals properly—something he has been learning ever since.

Soon after, he began work for an international chemical company conducting field trials for the Environmental Protection Agency. "It gave me an education about chemicals, but after working with the company for a while I realized that the test orchards we were working in didn't have any worms or other natural bugs because there were so many chemicals. After a few years, I put two and two together . . . this is some really bad stuff. Something's going on here."

He started working for Foster Farms in the Central Valley, running their chicken hatchery. In 2001, he moved back to his hometown and now works full time as the road operations manager of Mendocino Redwood Company, farming and ranching his eighty acres in his spare time. "We are not certified organic," he says. "Why do the paperwork and hassle with inspectors? I don't think I can charge more than I do now for our products, and I can't address a bigger market with my limited time. But, we haven't seen a drug, pesticide, or herbicide here in seven years.

"It's important to note," Mark says, "that from all my experience I can definitely say that not all large farms are bad, and not all small farms are good. It's tough to tell them apart. . . . People have a romantic view about agriculture and don't realize how hard it is. But we need a paradigm shift, to come together with our ideas to move things forward in a new and positive direction."

Blood Sausage with Heirloom Squash Puree, Early Girl Tomato, and Apple

From Michael Dotson of Martin's West

8 servings

8 8-oz. Pork Bangers, parcooked (see recipe below)

8 c. Squash Puree (see recipe below)

1/2 lb. Early Girl Tomato Pasata (see recipe below)

1 large apple, cored and julienned

50 parsley leaves

2 oz. Mustard Vinaigrette (see recipe below)

Preheat the oven to 400 degrees. Place the bangers in a large sauté pan with 2 tbsp. of butter. Put in the oven to heat through, about 15 minutes.

In a saucepot warm the squash puree while sausage is cooking. Toss the apples and parsley with the vinaigrette and season with salt and pepper. Place an ounce of the tomato pasata on each plate. Spoon a cup of the hot squash puree into the center of the pasata on each plate, creating a red tomato border. Place a banger offset from the puree and mound the apple salad on one side of the banger.

PORK BANGERS:

3 lbs. pork shoulder, cleaned of sinew

2 lbs. pork fat back

2 c. pork blood

1 c. grated onion, sautéed until soft

1/2 apple, peeled, grated, and cooked

2 tsp. grains of paradise

1 tsp. allspice

1 tsp. ground cloves

1 tsp. nutmeg

1/2 tsp. ground fenugreek

4 oz. heavy cream

2 farm eggs

2 tbsp. and 1/2 tsp. kosher salt

Partially freeze the fat and meat. Using a meat grinder, run each through the 1/4-inch plate separately. Chill again. Place all the ingredients in a well-chilled bowl and mix thoroughly. Using a sausage stuffer, stuff the mixture into hog casings immediately, twisting into 8-inch links that are approximately 8 oz. Bring a large pot of water to 165 degrees and poach the sausages for 45–60 minutes, or until they reach 160 degrees internally. Transfer to an ice bath to chill.

SQUASH PUREE:

2 lbs. heirloom orange fleshed squash, peeled sliced

4 oz. butter

1/2 tsp. ground coriander

1 tsp. fenugreek leaf

4 medium garlic cloves, peeled and halved

1/2 tsp. Aleppo pepper

2 tbsp. and 1/2 tsp. kosher salt

Place all ingredients in a deep baking dish. Place parchment paper over the top and seal with foil. Bake in an oven at 350 degrees until very tender, about 60–90 minutes. Cool slightly and puree in a food processor until very smooth. Pass through a double-mesh strainer and chill.

EARLY GIRL PASATA:

1 lb. Early Girl tomatoes

3/4 c. yellow onions, diced

3 garlic cloves

1 tbsp. gray sea salt

2 sprigs fresh thyme

Run first three ingredients through a vegetable juicer. Place in a pot with the remaining ingredients over low heat and cook until reduced by 50 percent. Strain and chill.

MUSTARD VINAIGRETTE:

1/2 c. extra-virgin olive oil

1/2 c. canola oil

2 oz. cider vinegar

1 tbsp. salt

1/2 tsp. fresh black pepper

1/2 medium shallot, finely diced

1 tbsp. whole-grain mustard

Combine oils in a pitcher and set aside. In a bowl, combine vinegar, salt, pepper, shallot, and mustard. Whisking vigorously, add the oils in a slow, steady stream until emulsified. Taste and adjust seasoning if needed.

Chicken and Leek Pie with Celery Root Crema

From Michael Dotson of Martin's West

4 servings

4 pieces puff pastry, cut into 3x5-inch rectangles
6 airline chicken breasts, from a heritage or free-range chicken
6 thin slices of natural smoked ham
18 baby carrots, blanched
18 baby turnips, blanched
3 c. leek ribbons, blanched
20 oz. cream sauce
Celery Root Crema (see recipe below)

Brush puff pastry with egg wash and cook according to manufacturer's directions. When cool enough to handle, split lengthwise into two rectangles.

Preheat the oven to 450 degrees. Season the chicken breasts with salt and pepper, then place a slice of ham between the skin and meat of each chicken breast. In a large oven-safe sauté pan with 2 tbsp. of oil in it, place the breasts skin side down; cook for 3–4 minutes on medium heat. Transfer the pan to the oven, cook breasts until just done, about 12–16 minutes.

In a saucepan warm the leeks, carrots, and turnips in the cream sauce until hot. Season with salt and pepper. When the breasts are ready, transfer them to a plate skin side up to rest; get ready to plate.

To plate, place a bottom piece of puff pastry on each plate. Divide the leek and vegetable mixture evenly among plates, placing it on top of pastry. Place a chicken breast on top of the vegetables. Spoon the remaining sauce around the plate, topping the chicken with more puff pastry. Serve with the Celery Root Crema.

CELERY ROOT CREMA:
1/4 c. shallot, minced
1 lb. onions, julienned
1 lb. celery root, peeled and diced
2 cloves cracked garlic
3 c. chicken stock
3 c. water
6 oz. butter
bouquet of the following:
1 tbsp. each coriander and fenugreek seeds
2 cloves
2 slices applewood smoked bacon
1 fresh bay leaf
7 sprigs thyme
salt and freshly ground black pepper
2 good shakes Tabasco sauce

Place the first seven ingredients in a saucepot with the bouquet over medium heat until all the vegetables are soft. Discard the bouquet and puree until very smooth in a blender. Pass through a double-mesh strainer, then adjust the taste with salt, pepper, and Tabasco. The mixture should be the consistency of a thin pancake batter. Strain again and chill. Makes more than necessary, but can be frozen for later use.

Forest Mushroom Haggis

From Michael Dotson of Martin's West

6 servings

18 slices "Haggis" or unmolded "Haggis" (see recipe below)
butter and oil
42 pieces hen of the woods mushrooms or other mushroom
3–4 sorrel leaves, sliced
30 small sprigs watercress
1/2 c. Mustard-Carrot Dressing (see recipe below)

Brown the haggis slices in a large nonstick skillet in butter and oil. Place on paper towels to drain of excess oil as you brown the hen of the woods mushrooms in the skillet. Spoon a line down the center of each plate with about 1–2 tbsp. of carrot dressing. Lay three slices of haggis on each plate, overlapping. Arrange the mushrooms over the haggis, garnishing with about five sprigs of watercress and seven slices of sorrel per plate.

"HAGGIS":

1 c. onion, finely diced
2 tbsp. garlic, finely chopped
1 1/3 c. dried mixed forest mushrooms, soaked in 12 c. hot water for 2 hours
11 medium button mushrooms, chopped in food processor
1 c. pine nuts, toasted
1 tbsp. and 1 tsp. ground coriander
1 tbsp. ground grains of paradise
1 tsp. nutmeg, grated
1/2 tsp. fresh thyme, minced
1 tsp. ground allspice
2 oz. mushroom soy sauce
1/2 bunch fresh parsley, chopped
3 c. steel-cut oats
3 tbsp. kosher salt
4 oz. butter

In a large saucepot sweat onions and garlic in butter until translucent, then add the mushrooms. Cook until no juice remains, then add all the dry spices; cook for 8 minutes. Add the remaining ingredients except the oats and bring to a simmer. Skim scum, then add oats. Cook 20 minutes or until liquid has been absorbed but mixture is not dry. Taste and add more salt if needed. Transfer to a sheet pan and cool slightly.

Using a sausage stuffer, stuff the mixture into 2 1/4-inch collagen casings (mixture can also be rolled in plastic wrap to same diameter). Poach tubes of haggis in water at 175 degrees for 2 hours. Chill completely before using.

MUSTARD-CARROT DRESSING:

3 tbsp. Carrot Chutney (see recipe below), pureed
4 tbsp. Banyuls vinegar
1 tbsp. whole-grain mustard
1 tbsp. salt
6 oz. grape seed oil
1 tsp. Aleppo pepper

In a bowl combine first four ingredients. Whisking vigorously, add oil in a slow, steady stream until emulsified. Taste, adding Aleppo pepper and adjusting seasoning if necessary.

CARROT CHUTNEY:

6 c. Nantes carrots, finely diced
4 c. leeks, finely diced
1 tbsp. garlic, chopped
1 tbsp. fresh ginger, chopped
2 tbsp. coriander
1 tbsp. Marash chile
2 tbsp. mustard seeds
2 c. white balsamic vinegar
2 c. turbinado sugar
1 c. fresh carrot juice
2 tbsp. salt

Place all the ingredients in a stainless-steel pot over low heat and cook until thick. Transfer to sterile jars and let sit at least 3 days before using.

Oakland & Alameda

Over a century ago, a young Jack London famously pirated oysters in this region while herds of cattle roamed valleys and hills planted with orchards.

The scenery in the East Bay may be very different now, but the quality of food used at the restaurants featured here has changed little, preserving delicious flavors of the past to mingle with exciting dishes of the present.

In 1976, Chef Rick Hackett travelled from Michigan to visit his aunt in Mill Valley. At the time, he was working as a "line cook expediter" at a place called Chicken Charlie's. This wasn't haute cuisine: "We would make instant mashed potatoes from the box . . . their idea of a vegetable was to open a can of peas and heat them up on the stove—still in the can!"

I'm sitting in Rick's new pan-American restaurant Bocanova, and it's a far cry from vegetables cooked in a can. As I sit down in a cozy corner of the bar with Rick, he begins to tell me his story. That summer in Mill Valley, Rick learned what California food had to offer. He went to his first French and Chinese restaurants and had his first encounter with California farmers' markets. That was the summer that Rick fell in love with cooking. "I realized I wanted to move to New York and go to the Culinary Institute of America."

After graduating, he moved to Washington, D.C., and worked for a "very French restaurant," the famed Le Pavilion under Chef Yannick Cam. Rick eventually moved out to California and got a job at Chez Panisse in the pastry department. Rick only worked there for six months, but during that time he experienced, for the first time, cooks giving the same care to ingredient selection as he'd been taught to give food preparation. He moved on to the Bay Wolf restaurant, where he met his future wife, Meredith.

In 1984, Rick and Meredith packed their belongings and took off on a two-year bike trip through Portugal, Spain, and France. Part of Rick's biggest inspiration as a chef was the time they spent in San Sebastian, Spain. Meredith taught English, while Rick visited local markets and looked for restaurants to work in.

The following summer in France, Rick remembers experiencing everyday farmers' markets that would be over a mile long. That's when he realized "how amazing we had it in California, that we could do the same things there."

Upon his return he put his new experiences and skills to the test in a variety of positions, opening and running a number of restaurants around San Francisco. He eventually became the executive chef of Market Bar in San Francisco's Ferry Building, which is literally surrounded by the Ferry Plaza Farmers' Market. One of the market employees came to him one day and said, "Hey, you have to check out Allstar Organics' amazing tomatoes." This is how he met Marty Jacobson and Janet Brown.

Rick remembers that "at that point, they were just farming a one-acre plot next to their house, but they had this amazing quality, and I kept buying more and more from them. One day Marty came up to me and said, 'I have access to ten acres, will you take everything I grow?'" Rick's response: "Sure, but how much does that produce?"

A few weeks later I drove up to their farm to meet Marty and Janet. As they sorted and packed for the next day's market, I asked what brought them to this place in their lives.

Back in 1993, "I was doing sales and marketing in a software development firm, and Marty was in advertising," explains Janet. "We started with a very simple idea, that we could live where we work, and work where we live." Marty jumps in, saying it was also "a chance to work for ourselves and bet on ourselves and our success."

From these seemingly simple goals came Allstar Organics, now a twenty-five-acre farm with four separate fields, each optimal for slightly different crops. On these fields Marty and Janet grow as many strange and wonderful plants as they can fit on their land; they aren't quite sure how many that is.

"Well, we have about twenty varieties of peppers, and of course the tomatoes."

"How many kinds?" I ask.

"Oh, we can't keep track—as many as we can, and it changes all the time."

They first started by digging up their backyard to grow tomatoes and herbs. The next year they were certified organic and sold their first produce. In 1995, they leased another half-acre, and more again the following year.

It wasn't as if the two of them had a plethora of farming experience, either. They reminisce about having to ask their new landlord, after leasing their ten-acre plot in Nicasio, Marin County, "How do you turn the tractor on?"

Marty wouldn't recommend the farming lifestyle to everyone. He laughs as he says "You really have to think a lot on this job. We've been doing this for seventeen years now, and finally, the five-year plan is starting to work out."

It's certainly working out for Chef Rick back at Bocanova. "I'm trying to get Marty to grow all the peppers I need. . . . It's our way of celebrating new world ingredients that influenced the cuisines worldwide, and what better way to do that than by using fresh vegetables grown by your friends!"

Pole Bean Salad with Dungeness Crab, Black Olives, and Red Pepper Aioli

From Rick Hackett of Bocanova

4–6 servings

1 1/2 lbs. pole beans, trimmed and blanched
1 lb. Dungeness crab meat
1 c. Peruvian black olives, pitted
salt and black pepper
lemon vinaigrette to taste
chives, chopped
1 c. Red Pepper Aioli (see recipe below)

Toss the pole beans, crab, olives, salt, pepper, and Lemon Vinaigrette in a mixing bowl. Spread aioli on the bottom of plate and mound the salad on top. Garnish with chives.

RED PEPPER AIOLI:
6 oz. rice oil
6 oz. extra-virgin olive oil
2 egg yolks, room temperature
1 tbsp. Dijon mustard
1 tbsp. lemon juice
salt
1 red pepper, roasted, cleaned, and chopped

In a mixing bowl slowly whisk the oil into the yolks. Add the mustard, lemon juice, and salt to taste (add room temperature water if needed to maintain the emulsion). Fold in the red pepper.

Zucchini Crudo

From Rick Hackett of Bocanova

6 servings

3 lbs. zucchini, julienned
1 pt. cherry tomatoes, halved
basil, chiffonaded
mint, chiffonaded
Lemon Vinaigrette (see recipe below)
Marash chile
salt
ricotta salata, seared

Combine the zucchini, tomato, basil, mint, Lemon Vinaigrette, salt, and Marash chile. Garnish with seared ricotta salata.

LEMON VINAIGRETTE:
3 oz. lemon juice
12 oz. extra-virgin olive oil
salt and black pepper to taste

Whisk ingredients together.

Roasted Banana Cake with Cream Cheese Ice Cream, Cashew Brittle, and Red Pepper Vanilla Reduction

From Pastry Chef Paul Conte of Bocanova

6 servings

ROASTED BANANA CAKE:

- 2 eggs
- 4 1/2 oz. grape seed oil
- 3/4 c. sugar
- 1/2 c. loosely packed brown sugar
- 3 large ripe bananas, roasted
- 1 tbsp. vanilla extract
- 1 1/2 tbsp. banana rum or any light rum
- 1 3/4 tsp. salt

Whisk the ingredients together in a large bowl until smooth. Next, sift in the following:

- 1 scant c. cake flour
- 1 tsp. cinnamon
- 1 3/4 tsp. baking soda

Bake the cakes in a cupcake tin at 350 degrees for about 20–30 minutes.

To roast the bananas, brush them with butter and sugar and roast at 375 degrees until golden brown.

CREAM CHEESE ICE CREAM:

- 3 c. milk
- 1 1/2 c. sugar
- 18 egg yolks
- 1/2 c. sugar
- 1 lb., 2 oz. soft cream cheese
- 2 1/4 c. crème fraîche
- 1 tbsp. vanilla extract
- 1 tsp. salt

Bring the first two ingredients to a boil, then take off the heat. Temper the yolks and 1/2 c. of sugar into the milk mixture. Put the mixture back on the stove to thicken up a bit, then whisk in the cream cheese until smooth. (Cream cheese should be room temp and soft before adding to base.) Next add the crème fraîche, vanilla extract, and salt. Finally, strain the mixture through a fine strainer and put it on an ice bath. Spin ice according to your machine's instructions.

CASHEW BRITTLE:

- 1/4 c. water
- 1 c. sugar
- 1/2 c. toasted cashews
- 1 tbsp. corn syrup
- 1 tsp. baking soda

Put the sugar, corn syrup, and water in a pot and cook until golden brown. Quickly add the nuts and baking soda and stir. Spread the mixture on a silpan or nonstick baking mat and let cool. Break up the brittle and garnish your dessert.

RED PEPPER VANILLA REDUCTION:

- Juice of 20 red peppers
- 1 vanilla bean
- 1 c. of sugar

Combine all the ingredients. Reduce the mixture to a syrup consistency, strain, and refrigerate.

Brown Sugar Kitchen

Chef Tanya Holland

City Slicker Farms

"There's so much family influence in what I do now," said Tanya Holland, chef and owner of Brown Sugar Kitchen in Oakland. "Even before I decided to get into this business, I was educated by my family about all kinds of food."

Born in Rochester, New York, Tanya learned about cooking from both of her parents. "My dad would explain things to me about cooking, and he showed me how to make a cake from scratch. My mom taught me savory dishes," she says.

When she grew older, she posted a Chez Panisse poster above her bed, "but really, it has nothing to do with the restaurant. I loved the artwork and didn't even know what Chez Panisse was until later." Her food world expanded exponentially when her parents started a gourmet cooking club. Each month a handful of couples would select a different world cuisine to cook from, she remembers. "Even though I was young, I remember clearly the excitement of all the different smells and tastes that came into our house during those nights."

When Tanya later went to college, she studied Russian language and literature. It wasn't until later that she went back to study food formally—this time in France at La Varenne Ecole de Cuisine in Burgundy. Attached to the school at the time was a "two-acre garden, more of a small farm really, where we harvested much of the produce we used."

Several years later she was working as a cook in New York when a Food Network producer approached her about doing a show. "It was really about being in the right place at the right time. But my French training really paid off then." At the time, she was working on "bringing soul food to a more modern state" and was asked to host a "Soul Kitchen" show as part of the Food Network's *Melting Pot* series.

Eventually tiring of New York, she made the move to Oakland, and when she saw an eclectic, triangular café in an industrial neighborhood, she knew she had the location for her next venture. "At first I thought I would just do coffee, some pastries" But her ambition got the better of her, and she expanded her plans to make it a full menu—morning, noon, and night. The Brown Sugar Kitchen was born, becoming a neighborhood fixture.

Over the years, Tanya has kept her interpretation of soul food increasingly reliant on the seasons by including menu items like dirty rice with seasonal vegetables. "Being organic, seasonal, and farm direct—this is the origin of soul food. Everything was direct from the plantation," Tanya explains.

It couldn't get much more direct than City Slicker Farms. In 2000, founder Willow Rosenthal purchased an abandoned corner lot and worked to create what is now home to a thriving community of fruit trees, a lively bunch of chickens and bees, and a dense and ever-changing perennial crop of herbs and produce. Originally an all-volunteer effort started by people who wanted fresh, healthy food to

come from within their West Oakland community, City Slicker Farms has now expanded to seven separate sites and produces thousands of pounds of produce each year.

One of the most extraordinary things about City Slicker Farms is how the farmers distribute their crops. From the beginning, the goal was to make the food accessible to those in the community who needed it most. To achieve this goal, a three-level pricing structure was created as follows: "Level 1—Free Spirit: Your unemployment check hasn't come, or for whatever reason, cash is not flowing in. Have some free veggies, no explanation needed. Level 2—Just Getting By: Money is tight, and if it weren't for City Slicker Farms, you'd be searching for deals at Safeway. Level 3—Sugar Mama/Daddy: You may not be rolling in riches, but you can afford to shop at Whole Foods or the Berkeley farmers' market. Pay a little more to help someone else out."

Executive Director Barbara Finnin explained to me that City Slicker Farms accomplishes its goals of increasing environmental literacy and self-sufficiency by installing one garden in someone's private backyard every Saturday and supplying follow-up mentoring for the new venture for two years. Over a hundred gardens have been installed to date.

I asked Barbara if City Slicker had other farm-to-restaurant collaborations. She replied, "Working with Brown Sugar Kitchen was our first collaboration of this kind. . . . Unfortunately, this is not our primary mission. We get asked all the time by restaurants, 'Can we buy your herbs, your produce?' And we say, 'Sure, but you have to come here to buy it, we can't deliver.'"

City Slicker Farms is en route to taking over two more city parks. In November 2010, the need for urban farming was supported, and City Slicker received a $4 million grant from the California Proposition 84 bond initiative to purchase 1.4 acres of land and build a new urban farm.

Herbed Buttermilk Dressing

From Tanya Holland of
Brown Sugar Kitchen

Makes 1 1/2 c.

Fresh herbs and buttermilk are a refreshing combination. Lately, we're serving this dressing on little lettuces or local chicory. Any soft herb such as basil, chervil, or dill can be substituted for a flavor variation.

1 1/2 c. buttermilk
1 c. spinach leaves, packed
1/2 c. green onions
1/4 c. fresh tarragon, chopped
2 tbsp. fresh chives, chopped
1 tsp. jalapeno, minced
1 tbsp. honey
juice of 1/2 lemon
coarse salt
freshly ground white pepper

Put all of the ingredients into a blender and puree. Season to taste with salt and pepper.

Collard Greens

From Tanya Holland of
Brown Sugar Kitchen

6 servings

Collard greens are synonymous with soul cooking in the same way that pasta is associated with Italian cooking. This robust green is the heavyweight of the cabbage family. I've replaced the traditional ham hock in this dish with a smoked turkey drumstick to lighten up the experience. The quick-cooking method here helps to retain this excellent source of vitamin C, and the dish has a low fat content as well.

4 lbs. collard greens, cleaned and large stems removed

4 cloves garlic, minced

1 smoked turkey drumstick

2 c. chicken stock

1 red onion, sliced into thin rings

1/4 c. cider vinegar

dash Tabasco sauce

coarse salt

freshly ground black pepper

Wash greens and set aside. In a pot large enough to hold the turkey drumstick, add the chicken stock and garlic and turn the flame or burner to medium heat. Simmer covered until the drumstick heats through and the meat can be easily picked from the bone, about 30 minutes. Pull out the drumstick; after it has cooled, pull the meat from the bone, returning the meat to the pot. One drumstick should yield about 2 c. of meat.

Prepare the collard greens by stacking the leaves and rolling them like a cigar, then slicing into thin strips. (This technique is called "chiffonade.") Add the greens and onions to the pot with the stock and garlic. As the greens wilt, add the vinegar and picked turkey meat. Season to taste with salt, pepper, and Tabasco sauce. Prep time: 20 minutes; cooking time: 45 minutes.

Brown Sugar Seasonal Fruit Crisp

Brown Sugar Seasonal Fruit Crisp

From Tanya Holland of Brown Sugar Kitchen

6–8 servings

6 c. of seasonal fruit, washed and prepared as necessary
(for example, if using strawberries, hull and quarter;
if using apples, peel and slice)
1 1/2 c. light brown sugar
1 lemon, juiced
1/4 tsp. cornstarch
pinch of salt
1 1/2 c. flour
1 1/2 c. brown sugar
1 c. oats
2 tsp. cinnamon
1/4 tsp. ground star anise
1 tsp. salt
12 oz. butter, cut into cubes

Place the fruit in a large bowl and toss with the next four ingredients. Allow the mixture to rest at room temperature for 30 minutes.

Mix all the remaining ingredients except the butter thoroughly in another large bowl. Blend in the butter using a pastry cutter or a large wooden spoon until the butter resembles small pebbles.

Pour the fruit mixture into a 9-inch glass or ceramic pie tin, or a square baking dish, or individual ovenproof custard bowls. Cover the fruit with the crisp topping. Bake the crisp in an oven at 350 degrees for 1 hour, or until the topping is bubbling. This time may be shorter for individual crisps.

Camino

Chef Russell Moore
La Tercera

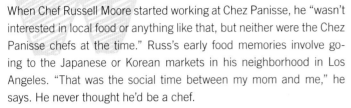

When Chef Russell Moore started working at Chez Panisse, he "wasn't interested in local food or anything like that, but neither were the Chez Panisse chefs at the time." Russ's early food memories involve going to the Japanese or Korean markets in his neighborhood in Los Angeles. "That was the social time between my mom and me," he says. He never thought he'd be a chef.

After high school, Russ went to community college but was "pretty burnt out by school, and then one day my car broke, so I stopped going." It was his mom who suggested he look into cooking. "At the time food wasn't cool, and among people I knew it wasn't even considered a career . . . but the LA Trade Tech culinary program was almost free, so I figured, why not?"

Russ got a job "in a really bad restaurant in Los Angeles" but wanted something better. A friend recommended San Francisco. "I was twenty-two and totally broke, and went around trying to get a foot in the door." The only people who were at all friendly to him were the staff at Chez Panisse where, after volunteering for one day, he realized he'd found his career. He says, "People have this perception that Chez Panisse was this wonderland of local food thirty years ago, and that's just not what [it] was." The focus at Chez Panisse was more "let's get cool produce like they're doing in Europe. I became the produce buyer and café chef at the same time, . . . [and] one of my jobs was to find what was not organic and to convert it to organic."

After working at Chez Panisse for over twenty years, Russ felt it was time to step out on his own. Together with partner Allison Hopelain as general manager, they took over an old furniture store and made the central feature of their new restaurant, Camino, a huge wood-fired hearth. From the beginning the focus was on the ingredients. "I didn't want to have a restaurant that shows off by buying caviar or lobsters."

At the beginning of each day, Russ compiles what will become Camino's menu for that evening. It's during this time that he'll suddenly wish he had more of this or more of that, and in order to get it, he finds himself at the Tuesday, Thursday, and Sunday markets. Russ is passionate about finding good produce and sticking with producers he trusts. However, he believes that "some of these chefs that are really well known, when it comes down to it, can't make the right decisions. They go back to buying cheaper food to make a profit. I just don't believe in that. As soon as you can get really good stuff from [a farmer], then you simply do it if you're committed to your craft." This is why solid working relationships with a multitude of farms and produce sources are important to him.

Farmer Annabelle Lenderink is one of these sources. "I've always liked to grow strange and unusual produce, but maybe because the times have changed, now I can grow things that people don't know about and they still buy them." For Annabelle, "unusual" isn't about

novelty, however. "I have to grow the unusual stuff because I can't compete with the usual produce, so I find things that nobody has."

Annabelle was born in the Caribbean, went to school in Holland, and eventually attended Tulane University, where she studied history. When she graduated, she started cooking in restaurants, where she was taught to make everything from scratch. She became interested in organic food, but in New Orleans at the time "there were only two farms that were organic . . . and one of them was actually more of a one-acre garden."

So, over twenty years ago, Annabelle came to California to farm. "If you wanted to be an organic farmer at the time, this is where it was happening." She got a job as an apprentice at Gospel Flat Farm in Bolinas, and, ultimately, she was asked to be a business partner. "Mickey Murch, who runs the farm now, was four years old when I first started there!"

In 1994, she decided to branch out on her own and started leasing various pieces of land, which she has farmed ever since. "At first it was challenging, with no water. I didn't want to do deliveries either. Anyone who was willing to come to the market and pick up from me, that's who was getting the stuff." Currently Annabelle is pursuing two jobs. She works for Warren Webber's Star Route Farm (see Chapter 2), and farms several pieces of land she rents herself in her "time off."

Not surprisingly, buying farm-direct is now more and more common, and hopefully it will one day be the norm. As Russ says, "I'd like to get to the place where we don't have to have that blurb at the bottom of the menu proclaiming how good all the food is or where it's from." He envisions a day when everyone simply knows the food is the best the chef can buy, no compromises allowed.

Grilled Chicken with Fresh Shell Beans Cooked in the Fire

From Russell Moore of Camino

4–6 servings

1 whole chicken
sea salt and black pepper
5 sprigs fresh summer savory (can substitute winter savory, thyme, or rosemary)
2 bay leaves
4 cloves garlic, slightly smashed and divided
4 c. fresh shelled beans (such as flageolet, cannellini, or zolfino)
fruity olive oil

Grilling chicken on the bone is the best way to get crispy skin and juicy flesh. Older breeds of chicken work especially well as they have thicker skins that take longer to render and crisp—with a boneless piece there isn't enough time to do the job.

Butchering the chicken: First remove the wing tips and feet. Next, remove the legs at the joint in the usual fashion. Then, with a large heavy knife, cut on both sides of the backbone. You should be able to remove the backbone, neck, and head in one piece. You will now have a whole breast on the breastbone with the first joint of the wing attached. Lay the breast skin side down on the cutting board, carefully place the knife along the breastbone, and split the breast in half. Save the wing tips, feet, neck, and head for stock or soup.

Making the marinade: Season the breast and legs with salt and pepper to taste. (This is best done the day before cooking.) Pound two cloves of garlic with a mortar and pestle until smooth. Pick the leaves of a couple sprigs of savory; add this to the garlic and pound until smooth. Add the olive oil to the mortar. Smear the marinade all over the chicken pieces and refrigerate.

Cooking the beans: Put the beans, two cloves of garlic (slightly smashed but not peeled), the rest of the savory, the bay leaves, 1/2 c. of olive oil, and a pinch of salt into a pot that will fit them comfortably. (I cannot stress enough how well a traditional clay bean pot works for this. Mexican, Spanish, El Salvadoran—pretty much any bean-eating country uses these.) Add enough water to cover the beans by 1 inch. If you are using a clay pot, set the pot near the fire for a few minutes to gently warm it up, then place it directly on a few coals (preferably next to the grill you'll be using for the chicken—no need to waste the residual heat). Once the pot comes to a boil, move the pot or the coals to bring the temperature down to a simmer. The trick is to taste frequently to gauge when the beans will be done and to correct the seasoning. Usually fresh beans will be done 15–30 minutes after the liquid comes to a boil. Once they are completely tender, pour them into something else to cool. It's best to cook too many beans, because they will be good for a few days after cooking them.

Grilling the chicken: Prepare a wood or charcoal fire. Pull the chicken out of the refrigerator at least 1 hour before cooking. When the fire has burned down to glowing embers, rake the coals under the grill. You are shooting for a medium-hot fire. Wait about 15 minutes for the grill to heat up and place the chicken pieces skin side down on the grill. Place a weight, such as a heatproof casserole or a clean skillet, on top of the chicken. After a few minutes start checking the chicken to see how well it is browning. Once the chicken is brown and crispy, flip it over to the bone side and continue to cook—this time with no weight. For a medium chicken that was brought out to room temperature sufficiently, the breast should take about 20 minutes and the legs should take 25–30 minutes. Allow to rest in a warm place for at least 15 minutes.

Serving the chicken: Once the chicken has rested, separate the legs and thighs. For the breasts, slide a small knife along the breastbone, then slide it along the rib cage. Separate the joint of the wing and the carcass. Cut the breasts in large slices and arrange on a platter with the drumsticks and thighs. Warm up the beans and serve with the chicken.

Sheep's Milk Ricotta Grilled in a Fig Leaf
with Cucumber and Herb Salad

From Russell Moore of Camino

6 servings

3 large or 6 small fig leaves
1/2 lb. sheep's milk ricotta (you must use the type that's formed in a basket shape, so it will hold its shape)
salt and black pepper
3 cucumbers (we use an Italian variety, but Mediterranean, Japanese, or lemon cucumbers work well)
6 tbsp. olive oil
3 handfuls of soft herbs (such as chervil, sorrel, Italian parsley, or mint)
1 lemon

Prepare a medium-hot charcoal, wood, or gas grill. Cut larger fig leaves in half and brush the shiny sides with a small amount of olive oil. Slice the ricotta into six pieces and gently place on the oiled fig leaves. Season with salt and pepper and wrap up in the leaves. Place the packages on the grill and cook on both sides until the leaves are a little bit burnt and the cheese is hot.

Meanwhile prepare the salad by peeling and slicing the cucumbers, mixing them with the herbs and gently tossing with the oil, salt, and pepper. Partially open the little packages and serve the warm cheese with the cucumber and herb salad. Don't eat the fig leaf—it gives the cheese flavor, but it's not great to eat.

Grilled Chicories
with Chiles and Lime

From Russell Moore of Camino

6 servings

- 5–8 heads of winter chicories (such as pan di zucchero, radicchio, escarole, or endive)
- 3–4 whole dried chiles (such as chihuacle, ancho, guajillo, espellette, or New Mexico)
- 2 cloves garlic
- 1/2 bunch fresh mint
- 1/2 bunch fresh oregano
- 3/4 c. fruity olive oil
- salt and black pepper
- chile relish
- lime wedges

Prepare a medium-hot charcoal, wood, or gas grill. Wash the chicories, halve or quarter depending on size, and toss with olive oil, salt, and pepper. Set aside.

Grind the chiles with the seeds in a spice grinder, or just break them up with your hands as fine as you can. Splash a couple of tbsp. of boiling water over the ground-up chiles to soften them a bit. Pound the garlic with a mortar and pestle or chop very finely. Chop the herbs. Mix the chiles, garlic, and herbs together along with a pinch of salt. Add 1/2 c. of olive oil to the mixture and stir together. If the mixture is very thick or too spicy, add more olive oil.

Grill the chicories on their cut sides for 2–3 minutes (there should be the occasional black spot, but not too much). Flip the chicories over and grill for another 2 minutes. Pile all the chicories together (still on the grill) and allow to steam for 1–2 minutes more. Remove chicories from the grill after they are mostly wilted and a little bit charred. Cut the root end off, spread out on a platter, drizzle chile relish over the whole mess, and serve with lime wedges. This is good alone as an appetizer or alongside other grilled vegetables, meats, or fish.

Eat Real Festival

Founder Anya Fernald

Marin Sun Farms

"After graduating from college I thought I would be a food writer," Anya Fernald tells me. "But I wanted to be a doer and an activist. I thought food writing would be too 'empty' for my personality." So she got into baking and cooking, and for a time she worked on a dude ranch in Montana, where she began to develop an interest in making cheese.

Upon graduation from Wesleyan University, she was so interested in her new passion that she got a fellowship to study cheesemaking for a year in northern Africa and southern Europe. After trying her hand working for *Saveur* magazine, she finally moved to Sicily to work on business development for a cheese consortium; it was here that she was introduced to the slow food movement.

Several years later, Anya began working more actively with slow food and started managing various slow food projects. She joined Slow Food International's publishing house, and before she knew it, she was program manager for the Slow Food Foundation and was asked to be director of the Slow Food Nation annual event. Ultimately, this 2008 festival attracted a record eighty-five thousand people who came to celebrate sustainable food.

"And then I became a radical in a way I hadn't been before!" she says. "What I mean is that I became much more aware of the balanced nature of the food industry around the world. People were having the same issues everywhere I went, and I wanted to help them with the information that I now had."

Anya founded the Live Culture consulting firm, which figures out "the business models that allow sustainable artisan food [producers] to scale up so they can make a little bit of money—this can't be an industry of martyrs. The people doing this amazing and difficult work need to find ways to be functionally compensated for it."

In 2008, Anya founded the Eat Real Festival, which has become an Oakland highlight. The festival combines the attraction of "a state fair, a street-food festival, and a block party to create a celebration of good food." The festival boasts 100 percent free admission and low-cost food booths, with food craft, drink, entertainment, and urban homestead tutorials on offer.

"I learned a lot by directing Slow Food Nation, and part of that was learning what not to do again," she reflects. "I started thinking about creating a street-food festival in Oakland, where I lived, as a response to how large and overblown much of Slow Food Nation became." And in a larger sense, Anya thought, "If we could start getting some of the street-food vendors in town to sell more sustainable food, hopefully people will start asking other people to do this."

One of the people Anya reached out to when she wanted to offer sustainable meat alternatives to the street-food producers she was working with was David Evans of Marin Sun Farms. It's hard to get more real when it comes to food than David. A fourth-generation rancher, he went off to college "certain that I'd be doing something

different when I finished," he says. But, ultimately, he returned and started looking for ways to improve on the life he led growing up.

First off, he realized he wasn't sure he could afford to have dairy cows in the long run—there had been too much consolidation in the dairy industry, and prices could fluctuate wildly. He wanted to be in control of what he sold from start to finish, so he didn't want to run a calf-breeding operation that sold to other producers. He decided he would start a 100 percent grass-fed beef cattle ranch. Leasing land from his parents, then slowly expanding around it, he now has almost four thousand acres on which to graze his cattle.

As a way to reach more customers while he slowly educates people about his grass-fed practices, David has developed a diversified sales structure. He sells directly to consumers at farmers' markets and chefs at restaurants, but he also sells through retail stores and a growing meat-based CSA. It's the CSA that started David thinking about expanding what he could offer; he wanted to work seasonally, to have product year round, but also to have a wider variety of products to sell. This led him to develop coproduction protocols, says Daniel Kramer, Marin Sun Farms CSA coordinator and director of marketing. "Now, in addition to the grass-fed cattle, we are able to offer heirloom pork, chicken, eggs, goat . . . these are all raised on partner farms around Northern California."

Walking around the Point Reyes ranch one afternoon, I see a creek running down the valley beneath me, a creek that contains one of the largest populations of endangered red-legged frogs in the region. It turns out that this is one endangered species that does better if colocated with grazing animals like cattle. Having a low density of grass-fed cattle on this land, as David does, is in this regard a significant plus for the environment as a whole.

Marin Sun Farms Bacon

From Chuck Traugott, Retail Manager and Head Butcher, Marin Sun Farms

1 quarter pork belly, around 4–5 lbs.
2 1/2 c. organic brown sugar
4 c. sea salt
2 tbsp. curing salt (also known as Prague Powder #1, easily available on the internet)
2 tbsp. cayenne pepper
2 tbsp. ground black pepper
1/2 c. organic powdered molasses

Rub each side of trimmed pork belly with bacon rub (created by mixing together the rest of the ingredients). Store in a container raised on a perforated insert or tray, and place in the refrigerator for 5 days. Remove bacon and rinse with warm water. Place in a smoker prepared with applewood chips, and smoke at 200 degrees for about three hours until the internal temperature reaches 140 degrees. Cool, slice to your desired thickness, and fry up in your favorite skillet.

Bread and Butter Pickles

From Michelle Fuerst, demonstrated at Yes We Can (a community canning workshop organized by Anya Fernald and Live Culture Company)

Makes about 5 pts.

3 lbs. pickling cucumbers
1 lb. onions
8 tbsp. salt
4 handfuls of ice

BRINE:
3 c. cider vinegar
3 c. sugar
2 c. water
1 tbsp. mustard seed
1 1/2 tsp. turmeric
1 tsp. coriander seed
1 1/2 tsp. celery seed
7 peppercorns

Slice the cucumbers between 1/8- and 1/4-inch thick. Cut the onions in half through the root end, then slice into 1/4-inch pieces. Mix the cucumbers, onions, and salt with the ice and set aside for at least 2 hours.

Combine all the ingredients for the brine and bring to a boil. Make sure to stir until the sugar dissolves. Drain and rinse the cucumber mélange. Pack them into clean pint jars. Ladle the hot brine over the cucumbers, leaving 1/4-inch headspace. Remove air bubbles, inserting a nonmetallic spatula or chopstick along the inside of the jar to allow the excess air to escape. Cover and screw bands finger tight. Boil for 10 minutes, then remove the jars from the water and let cool at room temperature. The pickles may be eaten immediately, but taste best when allowed to age for at least 2 weeks. Will keep for 1 year or more.

To make it spicy, add a hot pepper to each jar.

Baked Tofu and Veggie Banh Mi

Baked Tofu and Veggie Banh Mi

From Shari Washburn and Suzanne Schafer of Ebbett's Good to Go (one of the vendors at the Eat Real Festival)

6 servings

Our modern interpretation on the classic banh mi includes savory baked tofu and spicy Thai basil pesto.

1 lb. extra-firm tofu
3 tbsp. tamari
1 1/2 tbsp. white wine
2 tbsp. honey
1 1/2 tsp. toasted sesame oil
3 medium carrots
3 tbsp. apple cider vinegar
1 1/2 tbsp. sugar
4 c. packed Thai basil leaves
1 1/2 tbsp. fresh lime juice
1/2 tsp. crushed red pepper
2 tsp. salt
1 garlic clove
1/4 c. extra-virgin olive oil
salt and freshly ground pepper
1/2 c. homemade or good-quality mayonnaise
1 tsp. Sriracha sauce
Persian cucumbers, thinly sliced lengthwise
roasted red peppers, thinly sliced
cilantro sprigs
6 torpedo bread rolls

Preheat the oven to 400 degrees. Julienne the carrots. Toss them with the cider vinegar and sugar. Let sit for at least an hour.

Cut the tofu into 1/2-inch slices. Whisk the tamari, white wine, honey, and toasted sesame oil together. Pour this marinade into a shallow roasting pan. Add the tofu to the pan, tossing once to cover with marinade. Bake for 30 minutes and then turn the tofu over. The marinade will begin to char, but there's no need to add more marinade. Bake 15 more minutes. Remove from pan and let cool. When cool, shred the tofu using the largest holes on a cheese grater, or in a food processor. While the tofu is baking, prepare the other ingredients. Put the basil leaves, lime juice, red pepper, salt, and garlic in a food processor with a chopping blade. Turn the food processor on, slowly pour in the olive oil, and puree until blended. Taste and then season with pepper and additional salt, if necessary. Mix together the Sriracha and mayonnaise, adding more Sriracha if a spicier mayo is desired.

To assemble the sandwiches: Slice the torpedo rolls in half. Spread the bottom of the rolls with the Thai basil pesto. Cover the pesto with the sliced cucumbers. Pile the shredded tofu on top of cucumbers, then top with julienned carrots, sliced red peppers, and sprigs of cilantro. Spread the Sriracha mayo on the tops of the torpedo rolls, then close the sandwiches. Enjoy with lots of napkins nearby.

Pappo

Chef John Thiel
Alameda Point Collaborative

About two minutes after meeting Kate Casale, she is bent over chasing a flock of chickens between rows of broccoli. Finally grasping one, she tosses it gently back into its pen. "We just built this pen yesterday," she explains, "and they found their way out through a crevice in the back." Kate is the Growing Youth Project coordinator for the Alameda Point Collective (APC). In addition to being a chicken wrangler, she runs a one-acre farm at the west end of Alameda Island in the San Francisco Bay.

The APC was formed in 1999, creating housing and employment projects for formerly homeless and low-income residents on an abandoned naval air station. Today, there are over five hundred people living in the APC community, over half of whom are under eighteen.

"I was initially hired to do a community food assessment, working with twelve youth from the community," Kate says. "We spent the first year doing that assessment, at the end of which the teens involved came up with a bunch of recommendations—one of which was to create a farm on some of the land."

But creating even a small farm on an urban island surrounded by the San Francisco Bay was easier said than done. Kate spent over a year working to find the right location for their farm. "I had had my eye on this parcel for a while," she says, "but it took a while to get approval."

Finally in January 2008, they broke ground on the Growing Youth Project farm. When I visited the farm in 2009, it was already proving to be a huge success. In addition to Kate, there are a couple of other part-time adults and a larger number of part-time teenagers from the APC community working to run the operation.

From the beginning, the project had lofty goals. Primarily, they set out to change the food landscape in the urban "food desert" in which they lived. Without access to transportation, most APC residents didn't have a reliable way to buy fresh, healthy fruits and vegetables. The closest food option, according to one of the project's members, was a donut shop. And so the primary beneficiaries of the farm's produce are community residents, who can sign up to get a weekly assortment of the harvest. Any remaining produce is offered for sale at a weekly farm stand, and also offered directly to a number of local restaurants.

One of those restaurants is Pappo, owned by Chef John Thiel. Nestled on a side street off of one of the island's main thoroughfares, it's the kind of bustling neighborhood hotspot that might escape the attention of outsiders if it weren't so special.

John was born in Rochester, New York. His family moved to the Montclair district of Oakland when he was young. He started washing dishes in restaurants as a kid and hasn't looked back. "Work hard, play hard, eat good food!" is now Chef Thiel's motto for life. In addition to Pappo, he also owns Culina Deli inside the nearby Alameda Marketplace and buys from the Growing Youth farm for both locations.

"I first started working with APC when a customer of mine actually came into the restaurant and told me about what they were doing on the old base," says John. "Now I try to feature their ingredients whenever I can."

Before opening Pappo in 2005, Chef Thiel spent years working at a number of other Bay Area eateries, including Oakland's Bay Wolf. It was there, he says, that he first learned the true value of using quality local food. "The produce we got there would just taste better," he remembers, and he decided to expand on that idea when he founded his own place. "Here in Alameda, I was definitely one of the first making all these sustainable choices.

"You have a choice about how you spend your food dollars," he continues. "I could go to some big cavernous place to do my shopping, but when the opportunity comes to form a relationship with a place like the Growing Youth Project, you just have to take it."

A recent dinner at Pappo proved the wisdom of this decision. The food was simple and artful, and the preparation let the quality ingredients shine. Fresh crispy cod, for example, was balanced by the sweetness of Growing Youth golden cherry tomatoes, while a spicy pork chop was resting on the microgreens I'd seen earlier on the farm with Kate.

Back at the farm, Kate shows me the new brick oven that was just built the week before, as well as the framework for the sustainable aquaculture pond that, when finished, will raise fresh fish for the community. Both projects were suggested, researched, and built by local youth. When it comes to the future of food in Alameda, it's clear that the sky's the limit.

Marinated Summer Squash

From John Thiel of Pappo

8 servings

1 tbsp. shallot, chopped
2 tbsp. champagne vinegar (you can substitute white wine vinegar)
4 green squashes, medium to large
4 yellow squashes, medium to large
12 cherry tomatoes of various colors
1/2 c. olive oil
1 tsp. fresh thyme, chopped
salt and black pepper

In a small bowl, mix together the shallots and vinegar. Set aside for 15 minutes. Wash and slice the squash very thin lengthwise, by hand or on a mandolin slicer. Place in a large bowl. Wash tomatoes and cut in half. Add to the large bowl of sliced squash. Whisk the olive oil, thyme, salt, and pepper into the shallot/vinegar mixture. This is now the vinaigrette. Drizzle the vinaigrette over the squash and tomatoes and gently toss to coat all pieces. Serve on a white platter for a colorful presentation.

Marinated Summer Squash

Grilled Eggplant with Toasted Pine Nuts, Feta, and Mint

From John Thiel of Pappo

6–8 servings

2 large eggplants
salt and black pepper
1/2 c. olive oil
1/4 c. pine nuts, toasted lightly
1/4 c. feta cheese, crumbled
10–12 leaves fresh mint
Special equipment needed: **a pastry brush**

Wash and slice the eggplant into 3/4-inch rounds. Lay them flat on a tray and brush each side with olive oil. Season each side with salt and pepper. Place the eggplant on a hot grill and cook for approximately 2 minutes, then rotate a quarter turn and grill for another 2 minutes. (The rotating will help create attractive grill marks.) Flip the eggplant over and repeat previous cooking steps. If your grill is very hot, the cooking time may be a little less. The grill marks should be black, while the space between them should be golden or dark brown. Remove them from the grill and place on a serving platter. Drizzle with olive oil and sprinkle pine nuts, feta, and mint on top.

Simple Summer Gazpacho

From John Thiel of Pappo

6 servings

6 ripe tomatoes, cut into chunks
1/2 large cucumber, peeled, halved, seeded, and cut into chunks
1 green bell pepper, cut into chunks
2 garlic cloves, smashed
1 c. water
1/3 c. extra-virgin olive oil
2 tbsp. sherry vinegar
salt
hot sauce, for serving

In a blender or food processor, combine the tomatoes, cucumber, bell pepper, garlic, water, oil, and vinegar; process until coarsely pureed. Season with salt and refrigerate until chilled. Serve with hot sauce.

Berkeley, Albany & Walnut Creek

Known as the birthplace of California Cuisine, Berkeley is home to the best of the best among homegrown locavores. The restaurants presented on the following pages combine a passion for good ingredients and sustainable living with exceptional taste and variety, creating a food culture that upholds the area's history of culinary distinction.

Café Rouge

Chefs Marsha McBride and Rick DeBeaord
BN Ranch

Marsha McBride knows a thing or two about "farm-to-table." I spoke with her one summer afternoon while she and Chef Rick DeBeaord were grilling homemade sausages outside of Berkeley's Café Rouge. Marsha recalled a time back in 1998 when things were "very different," when this free-form style of roasting wasn't so highly regarded. Paul Willis, a free-range hog farmer from Iowa, "came to visit, and we cooked a spit-roasted pig out here on the patio in front of the café, and people got really upset about it." Now, "we frequently roast whole pigs on weekends, and nobody bats an eyeball," she continues.

Marsha began her career in criminology after graduating from the University of California–Berkeley. But after a number of years working in a high-stress juvenile dentention center in Oakland, she decided a change of pace was in order. She enrolled in the California Culinary Academy in San Francisco in 1983.

Marsha's career really started to take off when she began working for Judy Rodgers at the acclaimed Zuni Cafe. She became one of Zuni's charcuterie specialists and met Bill Niman when he started selling his meat there. In 1996, she opened Café Rouge, a restaurant and meat market, and was the first retailer of Bill Niman's beef. Executive Chef Rick DeBeaord, who had previously worked with Marsha's son, came to work for Marsha as a line cook at Café Rouge two weeks after it opened, and he's worked there ever since.

Central to Café Rouge's success are the butcher shop and meat market that serve as its core. The restaurant makes its own patés, mousses, and sausages, which can be used creatively in the menu. But the owner's approach is straightforward. Chef Rick says, "It's gotten easier and easier over the years to buy farm-direct. But really for us, it hasn't changed much. With straight-off-the-farm food, you don't want to do too much with it." That's especially true when it comes to Bill Niman's amazing grass-fed beef.

Sitting in front of the fireplace he built by hand, Bill Niman of BN Ranch launches into one of his favorite topics: environmental degradation. His views are entirely surprising. "One of the primary things we need to do," he says, "is to reduce the amount of meat we eat—reduce the portion sizes of the meat we serve, and eat it less often."

I'm at Bill's ranch just outside of Bolinas with his wife and son, who is playing with my daughter on this warm spring afternoon. Bill left the company he built from scratch, Niman Ranch, just a short time ago when he realized he no longer agreed with the policies the new managers were implementing. "It was just time for me to go," he says, "and start over with more freedom to do things the right way, not necessarily the most profitable or marketable way."

"One of the primary environmental disasters today," he continues, "is the loss of our topsoil due to farming, both here in the United States and around the world. There's a lot of land that should not be planted and tilled because much of that land is growing grain to feed

animals that don't need to be fed! One small part of the solution to this problem is the increased production of grass-fed beef. Let these animals do all the work, and reharvest the protein without hydrocarbon fertilizer inputs." Bill fires off more statistics about food production faster than I can type. He's a fan of pointing out that great-tasting meat comes from great pastures.

More controversially, he adds that grass-fed beef should be strictly seasonal because the timing of grass growth is important to creating the right fat ratio in cattle. "If you understand the cycles of the grasses and legumes," he points out, "then you can understand the energy cycle of when the legumes are highest in protein . . . and when they are mature and ready to drop, converting protein to carbohydrates." Based on this cycle, Bill has calculated that this year BN Ranch's cattle will be slaughtered on August 1.

Since Bill believes that the overall timing of the cattle's life and the timing of the grains' cycles are equally important, he doesn't follow the now-traditional rule of slaughtering fourteen-month-old cows—this is how long most grain-fed cows are raised, in stark contrast to past decades, when cows were three years old at the time of slaughter. But according to Bill, the younger meat in the market these days is "the result of cheap corn and cheap energy."

We take a stroll around his land, past the free-range turkeys to where some of his cows are grazing. These are younger cows, still a little small but certainly happy as they graze on the sloping green pasture. Bill stops to point out how the grass seeds are really natural, wild grain for his cows to eat.

"We're not pioneering anything, we're just reintroducing a proven technology that was used forever: the concept of truly seasonal, grass-fed beef."

Bavette Stuffed with Red Cabbage, Beets, and Crème Fraîche Dill Sauce

From Marsha McBride and Rick DeBeaord of Café Rouge

6 servings

3 lbs. bavette steak
1 small head red cabbage
1 tbsp. chopped garlic
2 tbsp. fresh savory, chopped
2 tbsp. fresh parsley, chopped
1 c. dry bread crumbs
2 c. red wine, divided
6 c. beef stock
1 yellow onion, chopped
3 lbs. red beets, chopped
1 c. crème fraîche
2 tbsp. fresh dill, chopped

Butterfly the bavette, seasoning with salt and black pepper.

Cut the red cabbage in half, remove the core, and thinly slice. Sauté the cabbage with a little olive oil until tender, then add the garlic, savory, and parsley. Deglaze the pan with 1 c. of red wine, then mix in the bread crumbs. Completely chill.

Open the bavette and place the cabbage stuffing on top. Roll up and tie. Brown in a skillet until nice and brown, placing in a baking dish big enough to be able to put a lid over the meat. Deglaze the pan with remaining the red wine and stock. Place the onion and beets in a pan with the meat, then pour over the hot wine and stock mixture. Cover and bake in an oven at 350 degrees until tender, about 1–1 1/2 hours. Remove the meat and puree beets and onions with the braising liquid. Serve with crème fraîche and chopped dill on top.

Three Bean Chili

From Nicolette Hahn-Niman of BN Ranch
(adapted from Deborah Madison's All-Bean
Chili, from *Vegetarian Cooking for Everyone*)

8 servings

*This is a wonderful dish for the cool, foggy days of winter. I always
try to make it a day ahead of time—it's best on the second and
third days. Also, I always use whole canned tomatoes. For this
dish I prefer them to fresh, and they're much better than pre-cut
canned ones.*

1 can organic pinto beans
1 can organic black beans
1 can organic kidney beans
4 tsp. cumin seeds
2 tsp. oregano (preferably Mexican)
3 onions, diced
1 tbsp. canola oil
2 tbsp. olive oil
2 garlic cloves, coarsely chopped
salt and freshly ground black pepper
4 tsp. sweet paprika
3 tbsp. ground red chile
1 large can whole organic stewed tomatoes, chopped
1 can Trader Joe's organic tomato sauce
1/4 c. fresh cilantro, chopped
dash of red wine vinegar
shredded sharp cheddar cheese, sour cream, and finely
   chopped cilantro for garnish

Pour the beans into a colander and rinse. Set aside.

In a large, heavy pot, sauté the onions in the oil over medium-
low heat until the onions are clear and their edges are browned.
Meanwhile, toast the cumin seeds in a dry skillet over medium heat
until fragrant. Add the oregano to the skillet for about 10 seconds.
Remove from the heat. Using a mortar and pestle, crush the cumin
and oregano together until they're quite fine.

When the onions are ready, add the salt, pepper, cumin-oregano
mixture, garlic, paprika, and chile. Turn the heat to low, stir, and
allow to cook a few minutes. Add the chopped tomatoes and all
their juices, the tomato sauce, and the cilantro. Stir. Raise the heat
to medium until the mixture bubbles gently. Add the beans and stir.
Simmer on low heat, stirring periodically, for as long as possible, at
least an hour. (You may need to add a bit of water occasionally.) Test
periodically and add salt, pepper, and chile according to taste.

Just before serving, add a dash of vinegar. Ladle into wide, heavy
bowls and garnish with cheese, sour cream, and cilantro.

Turkey Meatballs
with Escarole Stew

Turkey Meatballs
with Escarole Stew

From Marsha McBride and Rick DeBeaord of Café Rouge

6 servings

TURKEY MEATBALLS:

 2 1/2 lbs. ground turkey

 1 c. bread crumbs

 2 eggs

 1/2 tbsp. lemon zest

 1/2 c. brandy

 1/2 c. fresh parsley, chopped

 1/4 c. fresh thyme, chopped

 1 tsp. ground coriander

 1 tsp. ground fennel seeds

 1 1/2 tbsp. salt

Mix all ingredients and portion into 1 1/2-oz. balls.

ESCAROLE STEW:

 2 yellow onions

 olive oil

 2 heads escarole, chopped

 3 cloves garlic, sliced

 1 bay leaf

 4 1/2 c. poultry stock

Thinly slice yellow onions and sweat in olive oil until soft. Add the escarole, garlic, and bay leaf. Cover and slowly cook until the escarole is soft, then add the stock and bring to a boil. Add the meatballs and simmer until done. Garnish with chopped parsley.

Prima Ristorante

Chef Peter Chastain
McCormack Ranch

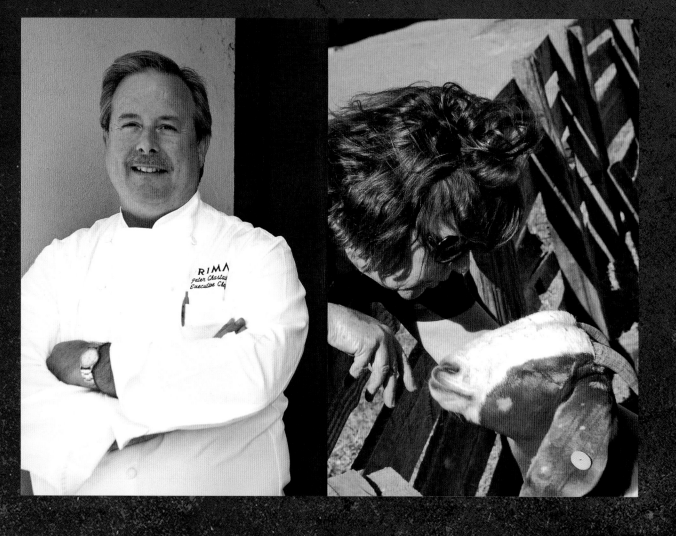

It's clear when you start talking to Chef/Owner Peter Chastain of Prima Ristorante in Walnut Creek that he really loves his food. One weekday morning I drove to Walnut Creek and was ushered to a private room in the back of Peter's restaurant. Very quickly Peter gets to the heart of the matter, saying, "You know, as cooks, our job is to rediscover the sources and to try to awaken people's interest in and consciousness around sustainability. I've seen how quickly our environment can be lost, and how quickly something we love can be destroyed if we're not watchful.

"In the 1960s I would walk with my father in the Berkeley hills, and we could see Contra Costa County with all the orchards out there, and he would say 'When I'm gone, it will all be houses.' That was huge for me . . . hearing him talk like that."

Peter was born in Berkeley into an Italian American family. "My grandfather had a large garden, and the importance of being able to provide for yourself was impressed upon us as kids," he says. One of his most seminal experiences was moving to Japan in 1978. The people he met there were "much closer to the earth" than what he was used to at home, and he became aware that even dense urban centers were fed by local farmers and gardeners. He became inspired to look for that experience when he returned to the United States.

The importance of time spent overseas is something he shares with Jeanne McCormack and Al Medvitz. McCormack Ranch was established by Jeanne's grandfather Dan McCormack in 1896. She grew up nearby in Rio Vista before studying at the University of California–Berkeley. After college Jeanne's path took her to Africa, where she joined the Peace Corps and eventually went to Harvard as a Ford Foundation scholar. She joined other scholars in the Harvard School of Education, where she started a PhD in education and later met her husband Al. Yet again, her journey took her back to Africa, where the couple spent two years in Zambia.

It wasn't until 1987 that Al and Jeanne decided to come back and work on the family ranch. They weren't expecting the increasing consolidation of the packing and grain industries. "The whole food thing is very alarming. The more consolidated the infrastructure gets, the thinner it gets, and the more susceptible it is to peril and outsourcing," Jeanne says as we drive from their Victorian farmhouse out to see their sheep and lambs. "The problem with the food industry in this country, compared with Africa for example, is that in this country no one has really gone hungry, so we don't culturally understand how devastating that can be."

When they first started farming the family land, Jeanne and Al tried their hand at organic safflower farming. This worked for about eight or nine years, until market conditions virtually removed the price floor. So they got into grain. Originally, the McCormacks raised sheep as part of a natural symbiosis with the grain. "The sheep gleaned

what was left over from the grain harvest, and it seemed like a good idea to buy more." Now they have 1,800 and are working on building to 2,000. "Because of all my travels, particularly in Africa, I was not hesitant to be a woman rancher where there are few, because in Africa, I had learned that women are the farmers.

"The locavore movement and the development of farmers' markets have been wonderful. However, the lack of local slaughterhouses prevents us from selling in farmers' markets." The McCormacks sell almost all of their lamb through Niman Ranch. It was Bill Niman who originally offered the McCormacks a guaranteed price floor for their lamb, something virtually unheard of in the industry at the time. This allowed them to continue raising their lambs in a highly ethical and humane way, without having to worry about costs.

That quality breeding translates directly into taste, which is why Peter Chastain loves serving Al and Jeanne's lamb at Prima. "We want to offer a diverse diet for people to eat," he says. "So, of course, we have the menu for the customer who just wants to eat a nice steak, but then we have the 'other menu' with the rabbit and fresh chickpeas and sardines. It's all the local, sustainable, wonderful food you can get in the Bay Area." Peter is also happy to assist in opening the door to new foods. "We love seeing our regular steak-eating customer switch to rabbit or sardines, and over time order the brain ravioli.

"I wouldn't call myself a political person," he muses. "But I have felt that connection through cooking. . . . I do feel that cooks are not artists or politicians. We're craftpeople, just like farmers."

Lamb Stracotto

From Peter Chastain of Prima Ristorante

6–8 servings

This dish reminds me of Sunday family meals eaten after jumping into huge piles of leaves outside while we waited for dinner when I was a kid. We would eat it with mashed potatoes, steaming bowls of green beans, and big lemony salads, then have pomegranates and gelato for dessert. The next day we'd get it as sandwiches in our lunches.

1 boneless lamb shoulder, or completely trimmed stew meat in large pieces

kosher salt

extra-virgin olive oil

3 yellow onions, diced

4 large carrots, diced

5 celery stalks, diced

bunch sage, leaves only

1/2 bunch rosemary, leaves only

1/2 bunch Italian parsley, leaves only

7 cloves garlic, germ removed

1 bay leaf

1 c. dry porcini mushrooms, soaked, cleaned, and chopped

2 c. dry red wine (Chianti is great for this)

2 c. whole peeled San Marzano tomatoes (including juice), seeds removed and chopped coarsely

freshly ground black pepper

1/2 gal. good, homemade broth, unsalted and hot

Season the meat well with salt and tie into a roll. In a large heavy pot, brown in olive oil on all sides. Remove and set aside. Adding a bit more oil, sauté the onions, carrots, and celery until the onions are golden. Chop together the herbs and garlic, add to the pot, then sauté until aromatic. Add the bay leaf and porcini next and mix well. Add the wine to clean up the pot, and finally the tomatoes.

Return the lamb and all its juices to the pot. Season with black pepper. Add the hot broth to cover all about three quarters of the way. Bring to a steady, slow simmer, cover the pot halfway, then cook slowly for about 3 hours or until tender. (You may need to add a little broth along the way or, conversely, reduce the sauce toward the end if there's too much liquid.) You can either pass the sauce through a food mill or leave it chunky—either way, serve plenty of it and pass on a platter at the table.

Leg of Lamb Roasted with Grapes, Figs, Honey, and Rosemary

From Peter Chastain of Prima Ristorante

8 servings

1 leg of lamb, thigh and round bone "corkscrewed out," shank
  on (not butterflied)
kosher salt and freshly ground black pepper
1 c. fresh rosemary leaves
1/2 c. flower honey
3–4 lemons
1 lb. green seedless grapes
1 lb. red seedless grapes
18 large ripe figs
extra-virgin olive oil

Trim out the gland often found on the inside of the leg. Trim any excess fat, but leave a nice clean layer on the top. Season the leg well with salt, pepper, rosemary, and honey mixed with a little lemon juice. (Be liberal with the salt and pepper—it will make all the difference.) Coat well with oil. Place the leg on top of the grapes and figs in a heavy roasting pan and roast in an oven at 400 degrees oven until medium rare—about 30 minutes. You may need to turn the roast once or twice during cooking to prevent the honey from burning.

Remove the leg to a platter and spoon over the "melted" grapes and figs. Allow to rest for 10 minutes or so, then carve it straight crosswise, from the thigh up toward the shank, into thin pieces. Serve with roasted potatoes or soft polenta. Be prepared to defend yourself should people attack you for seconds and thirds.

Fiery Lamb Polpettine in Salsa

From Peter Chastain of Prima Ristorante

6 servings

Although we say these are "lamb meatballs," they contain pork. The fat of the pork partly makes these addictive little bites what they are, but obviously the pork disclaimer must be made if one is unsure as to the dietary needs of one's guests. The other thing to let folks know is that they are not made for round eyes—these little suckers pack a punch!

1 1/2 lb. ground lean lamb

1 1/2 lb. ground pork butt, untrimmed

1 1/2 c. bread crumbs from good country bread, soaked and squeezed out

2 large eggs

1 c. Italian parsley, chopped fine

3 large garlic cloves, germ removed, chopped fine

1/2 c. fresh oregano leaves, chopped

1 tbsp. lemon zested/chopped fine

1 tbsp. dry chile de arbol, seeds removed and chopped fine

1 tbsp. white pepper, finely ground

2 tbsp. black pepper, medium grind (I use a mortar and pestle or a grinder—don't waste your time with pre-ground pepper)

kosher salt

SAUCE:

1 large yellow onion

1 large carrot

3 stalks celery

extra-virgin olive oil

6 cloves garlic

1 sprig fresh rosemary

3 sprigs fresh sage

2 cloves

1 tiny piece (pinky-fingernail size) cinnamon stick

3–5 hot oil-cured Calabrian chiles

1 c. dry white wine

2 c. meat or chicken broth

two cans whole peeled S.Marzano tomatoes with all their juice/crushed by hand

kosher salt and freshly ground black pepper

Chop together the carrots, onions, and celery on a board. Sauté them in some oil until the onions begin to turn golden. Chop together the garlic, rosemary, and sage. Add them to the pot and cook until the garlic turns golden. Add the cloves, cinnamon, hot chiles, and white wine. Cook for a few minutes until the alcohol is gone. Add the broth and reduce by half. Add the tomatoes with some salt and pepper. Bring to a steady simmer and cook, stirring occasionally to avoid burning, about an hour or until sauce is thick.

Mix the meats and the other ingredients together well by hand until the mixture begins to ball up and come off the sides of the bowl. Form the polpettine into small balls about the size of a large cherry. (It is important that they are small because they will pack such a wallop.) Place them into the simmering sauce and cook slowly until done, about 1 hour. Serve with risotto or pasta, or on their own with crusty bread and a salad. A good Vermintino from the Marché region of Italy is an excellent accompaniment.

Tara's Organic Ice Cream

Owner Tara Esperanza
Jacobs Farm

"Lemon verbena . . . I thought I had a bag of that, but instead, I had oregano. So I made oregano orange and pepper ice cream—I call it Oops!"

So begins my discussion with Tara Esperanza of Tara's Organic Ice Cream. At a production rate of six to seven batches per day, and creating over a hundred flavors to date, Tara's Organic Ice Cream is renowned for its herb-infused, creatively spiced, and near-genius flavor combinations.

Tara's passion for ice cream was a direct influence from her grandfather. "He was an ice cream addict, and every night after dinner he'd have some," she says. It wasn't until after college, however, that Tara realized, while she deeply loved ice cream, she didn't love what was available to buy in the stores. Five of her girlfriends bought her an ice-cream maker as a housewarming gift—everything else happened from there. "It started just for personal fun and recreation—I actually have no formal training in food," she admits. "I never thought this would be my business."

After starting Tara's in 2005 in New Mexico, Tara had trouble getting the quality ingredients she needed. She moved to Berkeley to get closer to the sources for her ingredients and to create a smaller carbon footprint. "I realized all the herbs I was buying were from the Bay Area, as was the Straus milk, and so much else. I just knew that's where I had to be."

Tara has been inspired by her many travels (thirteen countries so far) and has made it her personal duty to educate people. "It's really fun to watch people's expressions, since we really encourage tastings." With a degree in fine arts from the University of Massachusetts–Dartmouth, she relates the art of making ice cream to the art on her walls. "I feel like it's another form of expression and creativity. For my paintings, just like my ice cream, every color is mixed by hand. Nothing goes straight onto the canvas."

People come to Tara's to explore what Tara calls her ethnic melting pot for culturally diverse flavors. This, of course, includes the fairly unusual toppings. "I didn't want sprinkles and junk food, so when I first started the business I had a lot more toppings, such as lemon squares and tuile cookies. But nobody wanted them because my customers were purist about the ice cream." Now she offers more unusual toppings, such as red salt, virgin olive oil, and black sesame seeds.

"My grandfather passed away before I started this business, but I'm living his spirit vicariously through this venture." Though her grandfather may not have known the health benefits of an ice-cream addiction, Tara is out to prove you can have something really healthy and organic that's still amazingly tasty. "It starts from the farm, and the love they put into it, and the love I put into it. When people come in here, I realize, they get it, they really get it," she says, pumping her first into the air.

Jacobs Farm, founded by Sandra Belin and Larry Jacobs, was one of the main reasons Tara moved her business from Santa Fe to Berkeley. Jacobs Farm grows many kinds of herbs, while Del Cabo Farms grows tomatoes and vegetables and forms the other half of Sandra and Larry's farm operations.

In the 1980s, Larry and Sandra were overseas working in international development, offering fuel-saving cook stoves to people in Guatemala. After years of this work, Larry returned to the United States and decided he would need to be a farmer in order to understand his job as a soil scientist to the fullest. Sandra remained in Guatemala but returned a year later. Shortly thereafter, Larry left for a consulting job in Africa, leaving Sandra to begin the process of turning eight raw acres into a working farm.

"That land was originally all weeds. We had to machete our way to get to the garden in the middle of it," Sandra remembers, "and we were committed to not using any sprays to clear it—and we never have." In the past, Larry had had a bad experience with pesticides in the San Fernando Valley while growing trees in a wholesale nursery, so they had to remove all the weeds by hand!

Many years later, Larry and Sandra have turned Jacobs Farm into a thriving business, expanding far beyond the original eight acres. The original farm is still growing organic herbs and is their operations center, but a few years ago, they also started growing a wider variety of produce on the land, not to sell, but for their employees to harvest and eat. Community development is central to what they are trying to accomplish, and after traveling the world they have brought the concept full circle and planted it at home.

Larry says, "Fifty years from now, what we started will continue. The focus is on alleviating poverty; growing crops by making things live, not making things die with chemicals. We created a business model to help people generate income, not simply receive money from grants. And this will endure."

Tara's Organic Cajeta Ice Cream Sauce

From Tara Esperanza

8 servings

2 qts. goat's milk
2 c. sugar
1 large vanilla bean (slice the bean and scrape out the paste)
1/2 tsp. baking soda
1 tbsp. water

In a large heavy pot (not iron), combine the milk, sugar, and vanilla bean (add the whole bean as well as what you scraped out); place over medium heat. Stir regularly until the milk comes to a simmer and the sugar is dissolved. Remove the pot from the heat.

Dissolve the baking soda in 1 tbsp. of warm water in a separate bowl. Add the dissolved baking soda to the pot of milk. It will bubble up at this point. When the bubbles have subsided, return the pot to the heat. Adjust the heat so that the mixture is simmering briskly but not boiling. Cook, stirring regularly, until the mixture is a rich caramel color. When the cajeta cools, remove the bean and it should be thick. If it is too thick, add hot water; if it's too thin, cook it longer.

Baked Fish with Epazote

From Larry Jacobs and Sandra Belin of Jacobs Farm

4 servings

Flavorful, low fat, and delicious!

1 tbsp. olive oil
3 cloves garlic, minced
2 tbsp. red wine vinegar
3 tbsp. paprika
1/2 tsp. cumin
2 tbsp. fresh orange juice
2 tbsp. fresh lime juice
1 tsp. fresh organic oregano, chopped
1/2 tsp. salt
1/2 tsp. black pepper
4 6-oz. mahi mahi fillets
4 long rectangular pieces aluminum foil
1/4 c. dry white wine
4 fresh organic bay leaves
4 fresh organic epazote sprigs
salsa
lime wedges

Mix together the first ten ingredients (oil through pepper). Place fish in a wide, shallow baking dish and coat with the mixture on both sides. Cover and refrigerate for 1 hour.

Preheat oven to 350 degrees. Place foil on a baking sheet. Arrange each fillet on the foil, folding up edges so liquids stay with fish. Drizzle wine over each fillet; top each with one bay leaf and one sprig of fresh epazote. Fold the foil over the fish and crimp the edges to form a seal. Bake for 12 minutes. Remove the bay leaves and transfer the fish, unwrapped, to a platter. Serve with a side of hot salsa and garnish with lime.

Venus Restaurant and Revival Bar + Kitchen

Chef Amy Murray

Quetzal Farm

Chef Amy Murray, of Venus and Revival restaurants in Berkeley, grew up in Michigan, where she remembers the environment being "six months of frozen tundra and only three months in the summer of being delighted to be able to grow anything." Amy tells me, sitting in a booth in the back of the large Revival dining room, "Nobody we knew had a garden, but in the summer there were farm stands."

During her time at the University of Notre Dame, Amy got to spend a semester abroad in Rome. "I was just blown away by the food of Italy, and the family I lived with had a garden that we ate from. In Italy I learned that people were gardening for financial reasons more than anything, but it sure tasted good!"

When she returned home, she tried to re-create the dishes she had tasted. Her favorites were the simple ones like sautéed zucchini with spaghetti, where the whole dish was really about the good olive oil and garlic and Parmigiano Reggiano, which she brought back in her suitcase.

When Amy later moved to Japan, she "really fell in love with the whole possible world of food." Teaching English and living near a group of Japanese hippies who ran a food co-op, she learned to love simple and healthy country dishes.

When she moved back to the United States, she came straight to Berkeley. "Traveling and seeing all the farmers' markets and street food, the small-production mentality (which is pretty much all you have in the Asian countries I traveled in) and all the local and seasonal food were inspiring to me—and much of it, in the early 1990s, was still organic."

In 2000, Amy and partner Dave Korman opened up Venus restaurant. "We thought Berkeley was the be-all and end-all of the organic food movement." Because of this, they got more and more into developing a seasonal menu and working with local farms, figuring out different ways to feature the ingredients so the menu wouldn't look the same week after week.

The Saturday farmers' market happens to be a few short blocks from Venus, which prompted Amy to start buying foods from farmer Kevin McEnnis' Quetzal Farm. "Their stuff is awesome, their lemon cucumbers are the best, and they're just farming their land honestly, which is what we like to see."

Kevin has farmed in Santa Rosa since 1999, and his path to food was also inspired by his world travels. He majored in Latin American Studies at the University of California–Santa Cruz with a plan was to go to law school and become a human rights lawyer. After graduation he traveled to Guatemala and Mexico, where he was shocked to see the massive environmental degradation occurring—people were taking amazing rainforests and burning them down to graze cattle. This led him to study sustainable agriculture while he was in Guatemala, and he became more inspired by gardening than lawyering.

"When I returned to the United States, I went back to UCSC to apprentice with the farm and garden program." Kevin began looking for land he could lease to start his own farm and lucked into some land owned by the City of Santa Rosa.

At first Kevin tried to grow crops year round, until he realized how wet and cold his farm was in the winter months. He now scales back and prepares for early spring crops with little to no crop yield from late November to May. In 2004, he gained a business partner in Keith Abeles, who helps with the wholesale and direct store and restaurant sales.

Kevin has always farmed organically and is very open and transparent about his farming practices. He rotates his crops on a two-year schedule and selects crop varieties that nourish and are nourished by the soil he farms.

Among his specialties are the lemon cucumbers Chef Amy loves so much. They are the result of "lots of trial and error, and they ended up being a crop that grows really well that people really liked." After trying new vegetables and varieties several times a year for eleven years, Kevin realized that "diversity is a good thing, but we need to grow what sustains us financially as well as ecologically," so he has slowly decreased that number.

I spoke with Amy a few weeks after our conversation at Revival, this time while she was working at Venus. She had just opened Revival Bar + Kitchen a few months before and found working in the Venus kitchen to be a welcome break from the craziness that surrounds a new restaurant opening. She paused from her work to smile and told me, "You know, more and more I'm just really interested in trying to sell people on vegetable-based food," and then turned to one of her cooks and gave a refresher on how he should cook the squash dish on that night's menu.

Quetzal Farm's Lemon Cucumber Salad

From Kevin McEnnis

6–8 servings

There's no better lemon cucumber than Quetzal Farm's. I've tasted many. The skin on their beauties is slightly wrinkled, mildly pockmarked, with a deep yellow color. They are remarkably juicy and have a silky quality alongside their crunch. My favorite way to prepare lemon cucumber salad is with a zesty dressing of herbs and a good, thick oil.

6 lemon cucumbers, peeled, and sliced into wedges
1 avocado, cubed
1 hard-boiled egg, sliced
1 head butter lettuce, washed and trimmed into
  2-inch-square pieces
6 tbsp. lime juice (lemon is fine)
2 tbsp. shallot or red onion, minced
1 tsp. garlic, minced
1 tbsp. good Dijon mustard
2 tbsp. fresh dill
1 tbsp. fresh cilantro
1 tbsp. fresh parsley
1/2 c. almond oil (olive oil is fine)
1/2 tsp. salt, or more to taste
1/8 tsp. black pepper

Blend all ingredients together, whisking oil in slowly to emulsify. Taste seasonings to correct for salt/acid. Toss lettuces in dressing and arrange on plate. Gently mix other ingredients with dressing. Salt and compose salad.

Padron Pepper Salad

From Amy Murray of Venus and Revival

4 servings

This has been one of our most popular late summer dishes. People crave this combination of the mildly spicy padrons against the sweetness of the gypsy pepper vinaigrette, combined with the creaminess of good French feta.

VINAIGRETTE:

1/3 c. Gypsy Pepper Vinegar (see recipe below)
1/2 tbsp. minced shallot
2 tsp. water
1 tsp. sugar
1/4 tsp. kosher salt
Pinch of minced garlic
1 tbsp. chopped fresh basil
1/2 c. extra-virgin olive oil

Combine everything but the olive oil in a bowl, then whisk in the oil. Season to taste. Yields 1 c. vinaigrette.

GYPSY PEPPER VINEGAR:

1 red gypsy pepper, cored, seeded, and cut into 1-inch pieces
1 c. rice wine vinegar
1 tsp. sugar
1/4 tsp. kosher salt
1 tsp. sherry

Combine the vinegar, pepper, sugar, and salt in a small pot and simmer until the pepper is soft, about 5–8 minutes. Puree in a blender until very smooth. Stir in the sherry.

For the padrons: Rinse and dry about 3 c. of padrons. Mix with enough olive oil to cover, then season lightly with Maldon sea salt. Roast or grill briefly to get a little color on the skins, about 8 minutes at 400 degrees, or on your grill.

To plate, spread a pool of the Gypsy Pepper Vinegar on each plate. Pile up a stack of twelve peppers. Sprinkle with a good French feta.

The Sunny Side Café

Chef Aaron French
Gentle Giraffe Farm and Forage

Like many of the chefs I interviewed for this book, I never planned on becoming a chef. Growing up I was certain I would be a marine biologist, just like Jacques Cousteau. I spent part of my childhood with my mom on a small farm, and while I loved the fresh eggs we would collect daily, I admit to resenting having to clean out the chicken coop when my friends were out playing.

I'm a scientist at heart, though, so when my dad began to show me the science behind cooking, I started to pay attention to food in a different way—the thermometer, the ratios, the ingredients (yes, the ingredients came last for me as a child). When I asked him how to cook, Dad would research the most challenging recipes to teach me.

My mom and I would hand-grind flour with a stone mill that lived on our kitchen counter to make homemade bread, something I was ashamed of at the time because it made me different from everyone else. But without my mother's introduction to how it really was to eat fresh farm-to-table ingredients, I wouldn't have found myself working at the Ché Café collective on the University of California–San Diego campus during college. It was here, while also studying ecology and evolutionary biology, that I developed a deeper appreciation for the ingredients that make up our food. It was at the Ché Café that I was first called "Eco-Chef" as an insult by one of the other cooks, when I was trying to sort some recycling he was throwing out (environmental awareness hadn't yet permeated college campuses).

After college, I spent years working as a science teacher and research ecologist. After earning a master's degree in ecology and turning down a PhD program at Cornell, I realized I could never be content as just a scientist. I needed to express myself creatively and artistically, and in a way that was more tangibly satisfying. So I turned, once again, to food.

I have been the chef at the Sunny Side Café since it opened in 2004. Over the years, people have become increasingly aware of the connection between ecology and food, and I'd like to pretend it was due to a master plan, but honestly, it's simple serendipity that I've ended up working at the intersection of these two fields.

I find great pleasure in calculating the miles my food travels and printing the details on my menu each week. I love watching the seasonal pulse of these numbers, which creates a wave function over time.

Similarly, freelance foragers Mil Apostol and Lucy Collier, cofounders of Gentle Giraffe Farm and Forage, travel seasonally near and far to hunt the wild mushrooms and herbs they collect. When they walk through the Sunny Side door, I know they will be carrying some of the largest and most beautiful wild mushrooms I have seen, and I love to incorporate wild plants and mushrooms into my dishes to introduce diversity of taste and nutrition to my customers.

Actually, it was Lucy's parents who first turned the pair onto mushroom hunting. Lucy grew up mostly in California but also in

southern Mexico. Her parents are anthropologists, and the whole family spent every summer in San Cristobal de Los Casas until she was eight years old.

Mil came from a military family, moving around every few years. Born in Hawaii, she remembers some formative years living in Alaska. Her parents were always "eating weird things," foraging for berries and wild foods and fishing wherever they went. Ultimately Mil became a chef at Caesar after stints at Bay Wolf and Carter Brown Catering. "I've been cooking for twenty years. I wanted to do organic, local, sustainable foods."

When out foraging for mushrooms, wild herbs, and native medicinals, Lucy and Mil are conscious harvesters of the land, each using unique talents to aid the other in her quest. Lucy is the analytical one, good with maps and directions, reading the slopes of the land. Mil is the intuitive one and excels at finding the hidden gems once Lucy guides her to their general area. "We found that whenever you slow down is when you find the mushrooms. . . . When you let yourself feel a place, then you know where the mushrooms are."

Lucy emphasizes the need to treat the forest with respect and avoid pulling the mushrooms out. "Don't disturb the mycelium," Mil adds. The mycelium is the body of the fungus that grows mushrooms, the mushrooms being only the "fruiting bodies." Destroy the mycelium, and you destroy the forest's ability to grow more mushrooms in the future.

What I particularly appreciate about Gentle Giraffe Farm and Forage is that each individual mushroom they bring me is clean and healthy, with no small, dirty "fillers" bulking up the load. In fact, Mil and Lucy won't even pick the small mushrooms—they choose instead to leave them in their natural environment to grow and release their spores so more mushrooms will grow.

Wild Mushroom and Herb Breakfast Sausage

From Aaron French of the Sunny Side Café

6 servings

1/2 lb. wild mushroom mix (I usually use a mix of seasonal chanterelle, Hedgehog, and/or Black Trumpet—use what is good in the season)
1/2 c. olive oil
1/2 lb. ground heirloom pork
1/3 c. fennel seeds
1 tsp. powdered oregano
1/4 tsp. granulated garlic
1/4 tsp. paprika
1 tsp. dry basil
1/8 tsp. dry mustard
1/8 tsp. dry thyme
1 large bunch fresh sage, finely chopped
1 bunch fresh thyme, stems removed
1/2 bunch fresh oregano, stems removed

Trim and wipe mushrooms clean, washing only if necessary to remove sand or grit. Slice lengthwise into 1/4-inch strips. Toss lightly in olive oil and spread in a single layer on a roasting pan. Cook at 450 degrees for 20 minutes. Remove and cool, draining off any excess moisture.

Grind the fennel seeds in a spice grinder and mix with the other dry spices. Finely chop the fresh herbs with a sharp knife and add to the spice mix. Gently knead the spices and mushrooms into the ground pork until evenly mixed. Form into 2 1/2-oz. balls, then press into flat rounds. Cook on high heat in a heavy skillet until cooked through.

Wild Mushroom & Herb Breakfast Sausage

Carrot Cake Buddha's Hand Pancakes

From Aaron French of the Sunny Side Café

6 servings

This is one of the most popular pancakes at the Sunny Side Café. The recipe is balanced with the tangy bites of Buddha's Hand in the pancake batter.

2 1/4 c. flour
2 tsp. baking soda
2 tsp. salt
1 tbsp. cinnamon
3/4 tsp. nutmeg
1/2 c. sugar
1/2 c. butter
2 1/3 c. milk
3 eggs
1 1/2 c. grated carrots (about 4 large carrots)
1 c. Buddha's Hand, thinly sliced in 1/4-inch strips

Sift dry ingredients into a large bowl. In a small saucepan, melt the butter and add thinly sliced Buddha's Hand. Simmer on low for 15 minutes. Pour the melted butter into a second bowl, along with the milk and eggs; mix well. Grate the carrots until they equal 1 1/2 c., tightly packed. Place the carrots into a fine mesh strainer and squeeze out as much water as possible, then add to liquid ingredients. Add the wet mixture slowly into the flour mixture. Mix thoroughly until no chunks of dry flour remain. Adjust the thickness of the batter by adding more flour if necessary. (Both the carrots and the Buddha's Hand can vary in liquid content, which can affect the final consistency.) Cook in a lightly greased hot pancake griddle or pan, using 1/4 c. portions.

Meyer Lemon and Sorrel "Rhubarb" Custard

From Aaron French of the Sunny Side Café

In Berkeley, Meyer lemons virtually define winter California cuisine They grow here profusely in neighborhood yards, and week after week people bring bags and boxes of them to our door. Their tart complexity is nicely complemented by the tang of sorrel stalks. Look for the bright red stalks that look like rhubarb. I buy my stalks from farmer Park Guthrie of Wildcat Farmers in San Pablo. Park tells me that they are in the same plant family, Polygonaceae, as buckwheat and rhubarb. You won't find these stalks in stores—I suggest asking your favorite herb grower to leave the stalks on the next bunch of sorrel you buy. The grower is probably been throwing them away anyway! (If you can't find any, you can substitute rhubarb.)

- 1 c. Meyer lemon juice (from around 6 Meyer lemons)
- 1 tsp. Meyer lemon zest
- 1/2–3/4 c. unrefined sugar*
- 1 dozen large egg yolks (makes just under 1 c.)
- 1 c. sorrel "rhubarb" stalks, diced into 1/4-inch pieces
- 1 tsp. Cointreau (or other orange liqueur)

Meyer lemons vary greatly in acidity, which can affect the final custard considerably. Start with 1/2 c. sugar and season from there.

Start a medium saucepan of water on high heat, to make a double boiler. Zest Meyer lemons to yield 1 tsp. Juice the lemons until you have 1 c. (around six lemons, depending on size and condition). Mix the juice with 1/2 c. sugar and the diced sorrel stalks in a heavy metal bowl. Place the bowl over boiling water and whisk slowly until the sorrel starts to break down (about 5 minutes). Slowly add in the egg yolks while increasing whisking speed until all the yolks are incorporated and cooked to a light yellow. To the taste, it should not be "yolky." Add the Cointreau and lemon zest, adjusting sugar if necessary. Cool slowly with occasional whisking for a smoother custard. Serve with pancakes, French toast, or your favorite fruit.

Restaurant Directory

Betelnut Pejiu Wu
2030 Union Street
San Francisco, CA 94123
(415) 929-8855
www.betelnutrestaurant.com

Bocanova
55 Webster Street
Oakland, CA 94607
(510) 444-1233
www.bocanova.com

Boulette's Larder
1 Ferry Building #48
San Francisco, CA 94111
(415) 399-1155
www.bouletteslarder.com

Brown Sugar Kitchen
2534 Mandela Parkway
Oakland, CA 94607
(510) 839-7685
www.brownsugarkitchen.com

Café Rouge
1782 4th Street
Berkeley, CA 94710
(510) 525-1440
www.caferouge.net

Camino
3917 Grand Avenue
Oakland, CA 94610
(510) 547-5035
www.caminorestaurant.com

Center for Urban Education about Sustainable Agriculture
1 Ferry Building #50
San Francisco, CA 94111
(415) 291-3276
www.cuesa.org

Contigo
1320 Castro Street
San Francisco, CA 94114
(415) 285-0250
www.contigosf.com

Delfina
3621 18th Street
San Francisco, CA 94110
(415) 552-4055
www.delfinasf.com

Eat Real Festival
304 12th Street #4C
Oakland, CA 94607
(510) 336-6042
www.eatrealfest.com

Flea Street Café
3607 Alameda De Las Pulgas
Menlo Park, CA 94025
(650) 854-1226
www.cooleatz.com/flea-st-cafe/index.html

Martin's West
831 Main Street
Redwood City, CA 94063
(650) 366-4366
www.martinswestgp.com

Mission Beach Café
198 Guerrero Street
San Francisco, CA 94103
(415) 861-0198
www.missionbeachcafesf.com

Mission Pie
2901 Mission Street
San Francisco, CA 94110
(415) 282-1500
www.missionpie.com

Nopa
560 Divisadero Street
San Francisco, CA 94117
(415) 864-8643
www.nopasf.com

Pappo
2320 Central Avenue
Alameda, CA 94501
(510) 337-9100
www.papporestaurant.com

Piccino Café
801 22nd Street
San Francisco, CA 94107
(415) 824-4224
www.piccinocafe.com

Prima Ristorante
1522 North Main Street
Walnut Creek, CA 94596
(925) 935-7780
www.primaristorante.com

Quince
470 Pacific Avenue
San Francisco, CA 94133
(415) 775-8500
www.quincerestaurant.com

Range
842 Valencia Street
San Francisco, CA 94110
(415) 282-8283
www.rangesf.com

Revival Bar + Kitchen
2102 Shattuck Avenue
Berkeley, CA 94704
(510) 549-9950
www.revivalbarandkitchen.com

Slow Club
2501 Mariposa Street
San Francisco, CA 94110
(415) 241-9390
www.slowclub.com

The Sunny Side Café
1499 Solano Avenue
Albany, CA 94706
(510) 527-5383
www.thesunnysidecafe.com

Tara's Organic Ice Cream
3173 College Avenue
Berkeley CA 94705
(510) 655-5014
www.tarasorganic.com

Tataki Sushi and Sake Bar
2815 California Street
San Francisco, CA 94115
(415) 931-1182
www.tatakisushibar.com

Venus Restaurant
2327 Shattuck Avenue
Berkeley, CA 94704
(510) 540-5950
www.venusrestaurant.net

Woodward's Garden
1700 Mission Street
San Francisco, CA 94103
(415) 621-7122
www.woodwardsgarden.com

About the Author and Photographer

As executive chef at the Sunny Side Café (with locations in Berkeley and Albany, California), Aaron French strives to use local, seasonal ingredients in all the dishes he prepares. His studies of ecology at the University of California–San Diego and San Francisco State University, and his courses in sustainability at the University of California–Berkeley's Haas School of Business, reinforce his appreciation of a sustainable local food system. Aaron's writing and photography have been published by a wide range of print and online media, including *National Geographic*, *U.S. News and World Report*, *Gastronomica*, and *American Scientist*.

Elizabeth Tichenor is a California native who shoots food and editorial photography in the San Francisco Bay Area. You can see more of her work on her website www.elizabethtichenor.com.

Acknowledgments

Farmers, chefs, and restaurateurs are some of the busiest people around. Despite their hectic schedules, I was shown amazing generosity of time and knowledge as I traveled between farm and restaurant to research this book. To everyone in this book who took the time to show me around and talk to me about the workings of your operations: thank you. Without your support, this book would have been nothing but an empty shell.

I would like to thank my editor, Kari Cornell at Voyageur Press, who had the vision necessary to make this book happen, and Melinda Keefe for bringing the whole project together. I thank photographer Elizabeth Tichenor for her positive outlook despite dropped lenses and roadblocks of all kinds, and for her excellent attention to detail throughout the photography process that makes her work shine.

To my parents, Alfred French and Barbara Brown, thank you for teaching me to explore the world around me and for your unwavering support. And finally, this book would not have come together without the unique contribution of Elizabeth Sehan; I am forever grateful.

Index

Dedication

For my daughter Pearl: May you always be inspired by the bounty that surrounds you.

ISBN-13: 978-0-7603-3810-0

Library of Congress Cataloging-in-Publication Data

French, Aaron, 1971-
 The Bay Area homegrown cookbook : local food, local restaurants, local recipes / by Aaron French ; photographs by Elizabeth Tichenor and Aaron French.
    p. cm.
Includes index.
ISBN 978-0-7603-3810-0 (plc w/ jacket)
1. Cooking, American—California style. 2. Cooking—California—San Francisco Bay Area. 3. Cookbooks. I. Title.
TX715.2.C34F74 2011
641.59794'6—dc23
                    2011016684

Editor: Melinda Keefe
Design managers: Katie Sonmor and Cindy Samargia Laun
Series design: Ellen Huber
Layout: Pauline Molinari
Cover design: Karl Laun

The photos on the following pages are by shutterstock.com:
p. 1, Tomas Skopal; p. 2, Somchaij; p. 8, Shebeko, p. 10, Gary Yim; pp. 13, 87, and 152, Sarsmis; p. 37, HD Connelly; p. 43, Thor Jorgen Udvang; p. 83, Dream79; p. 97, Elena Moiseeva; p. 109, Jennifer Westmoreland; and p. 129, Anna Hoychuk.

Printed in China
10 9 8 7 6 5 4 3 2 1